Working with Sources

Exercises for
Hacker Handbooks

Working with Sources

Exercises for
Hacker Handbooks

Diana Hacker

Nancy Sommers
Harvard University

bedford/st.martin's
Macmillan Learning
Boston | New York

A Note for Instructors

The exercises in this book offer practice in key research and documentation skills: forming research questions, determining effective thesis statements, integrating sources, avoiding plagiarism, recognizing common knowledge, documenting sources, and identifying citation elements in sources. If you have adopted a Hacker handbook for your course, you are welcome to photocopy any or all of these exercises for a variety of possible uses:

- homework
- classroom practice
- quizzes
- individualized self-teaching assignments
- support for a writing center or learning lab

This exercise workbook is also available for student purchase.

After a general exercise set on forming research questions, the exercises are organized by documentation style. If you ask your students to use MLA style, see pages 3–48; for APA style, see pages 49–94; and for *Chicago* (CMS) style, see pages 95–140. Most exercise sets begin with an example that is done for the student followed by five or ten items. Some items are multiple choice; others ask students to revise. The exercises are double-spaced so students can revise directly on the pages of the booklet.

This booklet includes a useful answer key (see pp. 141–154). Students will find correct answers accompanied by instructive feedback—so that they will never have to guess why the correct answer is correct.

Using *Working with Sources*

Working with Sources is a tool that allows students to practice the research and documentation skills they will need for the writing they do in college courses. This resource supports students who are using any Hacker/Sommers handbook.

The exercises listed in the left-hand column correlate to the section numbers under the titles of the different handbooks. If you have questions as you work through an exercise, see the handbook section listed to the right of the exercise topic and under the title of the book you use in your course.

Exercise Topic	A Writer's Reference, 9th edition	Rules for Writers, 9th edition	A Pocket Style Manual, 8th edition
Research questions	R1-b	50a	25
MLA			
Thesis statements in MLA papers 1	MLA-1a	53a	29
Thesis statements in MLA papers 2	MLA-1a	53a	29
Avoiding plagiarism in MLA papers 1	MLA-2	54	30
Avoiding plagiarism in MLA papers 2	MLA-2	54	30
Avoiding plagiarism in MLA papers 3	MLA-2	54	30
Avoiding plagiarism in MLA papers 4	MLA-2	54	30
Avoiding plagiarism in MLA papers 5	MLA-2	54	30
Recognizing common knowledge in MLA papers	MLA-2	54b	30
Integrating sources in MLA papers 1	MLA-3	55	31
Integrating sources in MLA papers 2	MLA-3	55	31
Integrating sources in MLA papers 3	MLA-3	55	31
Integrating sources in MLA papers 4	MLA-3	55	31
MLA documentation: in-text citations 1	MLA-4a	56a	33a
MLA documentation: in-text citations 2	MLA-4a	56a	33a
MLA documentation: in-text citations 3	MLA-4a	56a	33a
MLA documentation: identifying elements of sources	MLA-4b	56b	33
MLA documentation: works cited 1	MLA-4b	56b	33b
MLA documentation: works cited 2	MLA-4b	56b	33b
MLA documentation: works cited 3	MLA-4b	56b	33b

Exercise Topic	A Writer's Reference, 9th edition	Rules for Writers, 9th edition	A Pocket Style Manual, 8th edition
MLA documentation	MLA-4 & MLA-5	56 & 57	33
APA			
Thesis statements in APA papers 1	APA-1a	58a	35
Thesis statements in APA papers 2	APA-1a	58a	35
Avoiding plagiarism in APA papers 1	APA-2	59	36
Avoiding plagiarism in APA papers 2	APA-2	59	36
Avoiding plagiarism in APA papers 3	APA-2	59	36
Avoiding plagiarism in APA papers 4	APA-2	59	36
Recognizing common knowledge in APA papers	APA-2	59	36
Integrating sources in APA papers 1	APA-3	60	37
Integrating sources in APA papers 2	APA-3	60	37
Integrating sources in APA papers 3	APA-3	60	37
Integrating sources in APA papers 4	APA-3	60	37
APA documentation: in-text citations 1	APA-4a	61a	38a
APA documentation: in-text citations 2	APA-4a	61a	38a
APA documentation: in-text citations 3	APA-4a	61a	38a
APA documentation: identifying elements of sources	APA-4b	61b	38
APA documentation: reference list 1	APA-4b	61b	38b
APA documentation: reference list 2	APA-4b	61b	38b
APA documentation: reference list 3	APA-4b	61b	38b
APA documentation	APA-4	61	38
Chicago **(CMS)**			
Thesis statements in *Chicago* (CMS) papers 1	CMS-1a		40
Thesis statements in *Chicago* (CMS) papers 2	CMS-1a		40
Avoiding plagiarism in *Chicago* (CMS) papers 1	CMS-2		41
Avoiding plagiarism in *Chicago* (CMS) papers 2	CMS-2		41
Avoiding plagiarism in *Chicago* (CMS) papers 3	CMS-2		41
Avoiding plagiarism in *Chicago* (CMS) papers 4	CMS-2		41
Recognizing common knowledge in *Chicago* (CMS) papers	CMS-2		41
Integrating sources in *Chicago* (CMS) papers 1	CMS-3		42
Integrating sources in *Chicago* (CMS) papers 2	CMS-3		42
Chicago (CMS) documentation: identifying elements of sources	CMS-4c		43
Chicago (CMS) documentation: notes 1	CMS-4c		43
Chicago (CMS) documentation: notes 2	CMS-4c		43
Chicago (CMS) documentation: notes 3	CMS-4c		43
Chicago (CMS) documentation: bibliography 1	CMS-4c		43
Chicago (CMS) documentation: bibliography 2	CMS-4c		43
Chicago (CMS) documentation: bibliography 3	CMS-4c		43
Chicago (CMS) documentation	CMS-4		43

Contents

Research questions 1

MLA

Thesis statements in MLA papers 1 3
Thesis statements in MLA papers 2 5
Avoiding plagiarism in MLA papers 1 7
Avoiding plagiarism in MLA papers 2 8
Avoiding plagiarism in MLA papers 3 9
Avoiding plagiarism in MLA papers 4 11
Avoiding plagiarism in MLA papers 5 12
Recognizing common knowledge in MLA papers 13
Integrating sources in MLA papers 1 14
Integrating sources in MLA papers 2 15
Integrating sources in MLA papers 3 17
Integrating sources in MLA papers 4 18
MLA documentation: in-text citations 1 19
MLA documentation: in-text citations 2 23
MLA documentation: in-text citations 3 27
MLA documentation: identifying elements of sources 31
MLA documentation: works cited 1 37
MLA documentation: works cited 2 41
MLA documentation: works cited 3 45
MLA documentation 48

APA

Thesis statements in APA papers 1 49
Thesis statements in APA papers 2 51
Avoiding plagiarism in APA papers 1 53
Avoiding plagiarism in APA papers 2 55
Avoiding plagiarism in APA papers 3 57

Avoiding plagiarism in APA papers 4 — 59
Recognizing common knowledge in APA papers — 60
Integrating sources in APA papers 1 — 61
Integrating sources in APA papers 2 — 63
Integrating sources in APA papers 3 — 64
Integrating sources in APA papers 4 — 65
APA documentation: in-text citations 1 — 67
APA documentation: in-text citations 2 — 71
APA documentation: in-text citations 3 — 75
APA documentation: identifying elements of sources — 77
APA documentation: reference list 1 — 83
APA documentation: reference list 2 — 87
APA documentation: reference list 3 — 91
APA documentation — 94

Chicago (CMS)

Thesis statements in *Chicago* (CMS) papers 1 — 95
Thesis statements in *Chicago* (CMS) papers 2 — 97
Avoiding plagiarism in *Chicago* (CMS) papers 1 — 99
Avoiding plagiarism in *Chicago* (CMS) papers 2 — 101
Avoiding plagiarism in *Chicago* (CMS) papers 3 — 103
Avoiding plagiarism in *Chicago* (CMS) papers 4 — 104
Recognizing common knowledge in *Chicago* (CMS) papers — 105
Integrating sources in *Chicago* (CMS) papers 1 — 107
Integrating sources in *Chicago* (CMS) papers 2 — 109
Chicago (CMS) documentation: identifying elements of sources — 111
Chicago (CMS) documentation: notes 1 — 117
Chicago (CMS) documentation: notes 2 — 121
Chicago (CMS) documentation: notes 3 — 125
Chicago (CMS) documentation: bibliography 1 — 129
Chicago (CMS) documentation: bibliography 2 — 133
Chicago (CMS) documentation: bibliography 3 — 137
Chicago (CMS) documentation — 140

Answers to Exercises — 141
Acknowledgments — 155

Working with Sources

Exercises for
Hacker Handbooks

Research questions

For help with this exercise, see the section on research questions in your handbook.

Circle the letter of the research question in each pair that would be appropriate for a college paper from ten to fifteen pages long. Remember that a research question should be focused (not too broad), intellectually challenging (not just factual), and grounded in evidence (not too speculative).

EXAMPLE

a. Why is the age of onset of puberty dropping among American girls?

b. Over the past two hundred years, how has the age of onset of puberty among American girls changed?

1. a. What is the current medical definition of schizophrenia?

   b. Which treatments for schizophrenia show the most promise?

2. a. What can be done to save our national parks from pollution?

   b. What can be done to combat air pollution at Grand Canyon National Park?

3. a. To what extent is solar energy an effective and economic alternative to fossil fuel energy?

   b. How many home owners across the United States use solar energy for part or all of their energy needs, and where do they live?

4. a. How have social media affected white-collar productivity in the American workplace?

   b. What impact are social media making on the business world?

5. a. How fair is affirmative action when used as a criterion for university admissions?

   b. When states have abandoned affirmative action as a criterion for university admissions, what have been the consequences to minority students and to the campuses at large?

6. a. What changes in social services were brought about by Jacob Riis's photographs of homeless and poor people in New York City at the end of the nineteenth century?

   b. What social services were available in New York City at the end of the nineteenth century?

7. a. What laws have been passed to regulate the ways in which farmers cultivate and harvest their crops?

   b. Why should the US government allow farmers to sell genetically engineered produce?

8. a. How can pharmaceutical companies be encouraged to provide low-cost drugs to combat AIDS in Africa?

   b. What drugs are desperately needed to combat AIDS in Africa?

9. a. What is morally wrong with allowing prayer—or at least a moment of silence—in public schools?

   b. On what legal grounds has the Supreme Court refused to allow official prayer in public schools, and how has its decision affected elementary education?

10. a. What are the provisions of Title IX, the 1972 act that banned gender discrimination in publicly funded US schools?

    b. How has Title IX, which has banned gender discrimination in publicly funded US schools since 1972, affected college athletic programs?

Hacker/Sommers, *Working with Sources: Exercises for Hacker Handbooks* (Boston: Bedford, 2018)

Thesis statements in MLA papers 1

For help with this exercise, see the section on thesis statements in MLA papers in your handbook.

Circle the letter of the sentence in each pair that would work well as the thesis statement for a research paper of about ten pages. Remember that a thesis should be a central idea that requires supporting evidence, it should be of adequate scope for a ten-page paper, and it should be sharply focused.

EXAMPLE

a. Although Thurgood Marshall and Martin Luther King, Jr., agreed that integration was a central goal of the civil rights movement, they did not agree on the methods of achieving it.

b. Civil rights leaders Thurgood Marshall and Martin Luther King, Jr., were similar in many ways, but they had differences, too.

1. a. Residents of the District of Columbia must pay federal income taxes, even though they are denied voting representation in the US Congress.

   b. Residents of the District of Columbia should have voting representation in Congress because they pay federal income taxes.

2. a. Why do young people have a fascination with vampires?

   b. The fascination with vampires among young people reflects our cultural obsession with immortality, youth, and individuality.

3. a. Political and economic conditions in the early twentieth century help explain the popularity of Marcus Garvey's Back to Africa movement.

   b. Marcus Garvey founded the Universal Negro Improvement Association and initiated the popular Back to Africa movement.

4. a. Because fighting terrorists who plan their activities online is a high priority for the US government, Congress should enact laws that limit computer privacy and allow for wiretapping and other forms of surveillance.

   b. American citizens must give up their privacy rights so that the US government can find and convict political terrorists.

5. a. As the public becomes increasingly aware of elite athletes using performance-enhancing drugs, people must reconsider what it means to be a hero.

   b. If an elite athlete is driven to succeed at all costs, perhaps the twenty-first-century hero should be a new model, one who prizes honor above success and strives to *be* good rather than to simply *look* good.

6. a. Seasonal affective disorder, common in northern countries such as Norway and Sweden, is a debilitating condition that affects many people during the winter months.

   b. Because light therapy and antidepressants do not always help those suffering from seasonal affective disorder, patients should also consider making dietary changes and taking supplements.

7. a. Throughout history, big-business interests have almost always been at odds with environmentally friendly practices.

   b. Although big businesses have traditionally been at odds with environmental interests, eco-friendly policies can actually lead to increased corporate profits.

8. a. In April of 2009, the US government declared the H1N1 flu virus, which originated in Mexico, a public health emergency and responded with both a vaccination plan and a public outreach campaign.

   b. A close look at the H1N1 flu virus epidemic of 2009, which originated in Mexico, reveals an unfairly racist response from the US government, the American media, and the American people.

9. a. The phrase "separation of church and state" does not appear in the US Constitution; Thomas Jefferson coined it in a famous letter explaining the First Amendment.

   b. Americans must continue to maintain the separation of church and state to protect religious minorities and to protect religion itself from domination by the state.

10. a. To write a film based on a book, screenwriters must pay attention to length, narration, visual appeal, and nuance, all of which make it difficult to remain true to the source material.

    b. *The Hunger Games* books were better than the movies, as is common when books are converted into films.

Hacker/Sommers, *Working with Sources: Exercises for Hacker Handbooks* (Boston: Bedford, 2018)

Thesis statements in MLA papers 2

For help with this exercise, see the section on thesis statements in MLA papers in your handbook.

Circle the letter of the sentence in each pair that would work well as the thesis statement for a research paper of about ten pages. Remember that a thesis should be a central idea that requires supporting evidence; it should be of adequate scope for a ten-page paper; and it should be sharply focused. Be prepared to explain your answer.

EXAMPLE

a. The need for universal health care in the United States is more urgent than ever.

(b.) Universal health care would be an improvement over the current US health care system in terms of economics, access to care, and quality of care.

1. a. Legislators should not reinstate the Fairness Doctrine, which required broadcasters to provide balanced coverage of controversial topics; this federal policy had the negative effect of watering down political debate.

   b. The Federal Communications Commission abolished the Fairness Doctrine, a federal policy that required broadcasters to provide balanced coverage of controversial topics, in 1987.

2. a. While reality shows might provide entertainment, scripted television is an art form, as it cultivates plot, showcases acting talent, and controls variables such as lighting, sound, and camera angles.

   b. There are many reasons that scripted television is better than reality television.

3. a. What is it about the Olympic Games that attracts potential host cities?

   b. Host nations, often seeking economic benefits and civic pride, must make better plans to offset the environmental costs of hosting the Olympic Games.

4. a. More than one-third of the cumulative carbon dioxide emissions over the past century can be attributed to deforestation.

   b. Although much of the discussion about carbon dioxide emissions focuses on automobiles and factories, one of the most efficient ways of cutting emissions is through forest restoration and conservation.

5. a. While SAT scores are fairly accurate at predicting the academic success rates of white students, they are very poor at predicting the academic success rates of minority students.

   b. SAT scores should be eliminated from college admissions requirements because they do not accurately predict the academic success rates of minority students.

6. a. Although *Catch-22* is set during World War II, Joseph Heller uses the novel to comment on the absurdity of Cold War society.

   b. Joseph Heller's novel *Catch-22* led to the widespread use of the term *catch-22*, which refers to a paradox or a situation that cannot be escaped with a desirable outcome.

7. a. To prepare students to live on their own after high school, school districts should fund and require a course that covers personal banking, insurance basics, and money management for all students in twelfth grade.

   b. Students aren't prepared to live on their own after high school, but is it their fault?

8. a. Public schools should consider the benefits of mandatory religious education, which can lead to increased tolerance of religious views.

   b. Religious education in public schools is a controversial topic, mostly because the First Amendment guarantee of freedom of religion has led to a separation of church and state.

9. a. Although the Civil Rights Act of 1964 guarantees workers the right to equal pay regardless of race, sex, religion, or ethnicity, more stringent laws are needed because the current law contains loopholes that allow unfair pay practices to continue.

   b. The Civil Rights Act of 1964 provided for the creation of the Equal Employment Opportunity Commission (EEOC), which, among other things, guarantees employees equal pay, regardless of race, sex, religion, or ethnicity.

10. a. Recording artist David Bowie was a quirky musician beloved by gay, straight, and transgender fans around the world.

    b. Recording artist David Bowie did more to challenge gender norms and to empower LGBTQ youth than any legislation passed during his lifetime.

Hacker/Sommers, *Working with Sources: Exercises for Hacker Handbooks* (Boston: Bedford, 2018)

Avoiding plagiarism in MLA papers 1

For help with this exercise, see the section on avoiding plagiarism in MLA papers in your handbook.

Read the following passage and the information about its source. Then decide whether each student sample is plagiarized or uses the source correctly. If the student's sample is plagiarized, write "plagiarized"; if the sample is acceptable, write "OK."

ORIGINAL SOURCE

> Smartphone games are built on a very different model [from traditional video games]. The iPhone's screen is roughly the size of a playing card; it responds not to the fast-twitch button combos of a controller but to more intuitive and intimate motions: poking, pinching, tapping, tickling. This has encouraged a very different kind of game: Tetris-like little puzzles, broken into discrete bits, designed to be played anywhere, in any context, without a manual, by any level of player. (Charles Pratt, a researcher in New York University's Game Center, refers to such games as "knitting games.") You could argue that these are pure games: perfectly designed minisystems engineered to take us directly to the core of gaming pleasure without the distraction of narrative.
>
> From Anderson, Sam. "Just One More Game. . . ." *The New York Times Magazine*, 4 Apr. 2012, nyti.ms/1AZ2pys.

1. Smartphone screens have encouraged a new type of intimate game, broken into discrete bits, that can be played by anyone, anywhere.

2. The smartphone touchscreen has changed the nature of video games: instead of "fast-twitch button combos," touchscreens use "intuitive and intimate motions" such as "poking [and] pinching" (Anderson).

3. As Sam Anderson explains, games on smartphones are "designed to be played anywhere, in any context, without a manual, by any level of player."

4. Sam Anderson points out that, unlike older, narrative-based games that required a controller, games played on smartphone touchscreens can be learned quickly by anyone, regardless of skill level.

5. Smartphone games can be called "perfectly designed minisystems" because they bring us right into the game "without the distraction of narrative."

Avoiding plagiarism in MLA papers 2

For help with this exercise, see the section on avoiding plagiarism in MLA papers in your handbook.

Read the following passage and the information about its source. Then decide whether each student sample is plagiarized or uses the source correctly. If the student's sample is plagiarized, write "plagiarized"; if the sample is acceptable, write "OK."

ORIGINAL SOURCE

We probably spend more time thinking and talking about other people than anything else. If another person makes us exuberantly happy, furiously angry, or deeply sad, we often can't stop thinking about him or her. We will often drop his or her name in our conversations with others, tossing in numerous pronouns as we refer to the person. Consequently, if the speaker is thinking and talking about a friend, expect high rates of third-person singular pronouns. If worried about communists, right-wing radio hosts, or bureaucrats, words such as *they* and *them* will be more frequent than average.

The word *I* is no different. If people are self-conscious, their attention flips to themselves briefly but at higher rates than people who are not self-conscious. For example, people use the word *I* more when completing a questionnaire in front of a mirror than if no mirror is present. If their attention is drawn to themselves because they are sick, feeling pain, or deeply depressed, they also use *I* more. In contrast, people who are immersed in a task tend to use I-words at very low levels.

From Pennebaker, James W. *The Secret Life of Pronouns: What Our Words Say about Us.* Bloomsbury Press, 2011. [The source passage is from pages 291-92. Page 291 ends after *Consequently*, at the start of the fourth sentence.]

1. Adults spend more time thinking and talking about other people than they spend on anything else.

2. High levels of emotion about someone may cause us to refer to that person more often and to use "numerous pronouns as we refer to the person" (Pennebaker 291).

3. Pennebaker notes that people talking about friends will use "high rates of third-person singular pronouns," whereas plural pronouns "such as *they* and *them* will be more frequent than average" when people are talking about certain groups that might make them uncomfortable (292).

4. Pennebaker explains that self-conscious people use *I* more often because "their attention flips to themselves at higher rates than people who are not self-conscious" (292).

5. Pennebaker suggests that we can understand the way speakers regard those whom they are talking about by analyzing the pronouns the speakers use most frequently (291-92).

Hacker/Sommers, *Working with Sources: Exercises for Hacker Handbooks* (Boston: Bedford, 2018)

Avoiding plagiarism in MLA papers 3

For help with this exercise, see the section on avoiding plagiarism in MLA papers in your handbook.

Read the following passage and the information about its source. Then decide whether each student sample is plagiarized or uses the source correctly. If the student sample is plagiarized, write "plagiarized"; if the sample is acceptable, write "OK."

ORIGINAL SOURCE

Apart from the fact that music accounts for much of the power of Hindi movies, creating a heightened mood that dialogue can rarely achieve, the film song spreads out from cinema to permeate many other areas of Indian society. Even before the advent of cheap audiocassettes, in the days when record players were rare and expensive, film songs achieved far-reaching popularity through street singers and wedding bands, which often played film hits rather than folk or traditional tunes. And the songs, with their inventive Hindi/Urdu lyrics (often written by celebrated poets), have long been a bonding force in the Indian diaspora, re-creating a familiar world of images and emotions and linking millions of people to their homeland.

From Kabir, Nasreen Munni. "Playback Time: A Brief History of Bollywood 'Film Songs.'" *Film Comment*, May-June 2002, pp. 41-43. [The source passage is from page 41.]

1. In India, film music creates a heightened mood that accounts for a great deal of the power of Hindi movies, writes Nasreen Munni Kabir (41).

2. Nasreen Munni Kabir argues that the film songs disseminate from the movies to pervade several other aspects of Indian life (41).

3. Nasreen Munni Kabir notes that the songs in Hindi movies became widely popular even when few Indians owned recordings (41).

4. As Nasreen Munni Kabir explains, Hindi film songs managed to reach a broad audience "before the advent of cheap audiocassettes, in the days when record players were rare and expensive" (41).

5. Street singers and wedding performers helped film songs achieve far-reaching popularity, according to Nasreen Munni Kabir (41).

6. Nasreen Munni Kabir points out that Hindi film songs not only contribute significantly to the effectiveness of the films in which they appear but also attract a worldwide audience of Indians who use them to reconnect to their roots and their communities (41).

7. In Hindi films, the songs have inventive Hindi/Urdu lyrics that are often written by celebrated poets.

8. According to Nasreen Munni Kabir, music in Hindi films pervades the culture both in India and abroad as it presents "a familiar world of images and emotions" (41).

9. Hindi film songs have long re-created a familiar world of images and emotions to link millions of Indians to their homeland.

10. Nasreen Munni Kabir believes that the beloved songs in Indian films have been "a bonding force in the Indian diaspora" (41).

Hacker/Sommers, *Working with Sources: Exercises for Hacker Handbooks* (Boston: Bedford, 2018)

Avoiding plagiarism in MLA papers 4

For help with this exercise, see the section on avoiding plagiarism in MLA papers in your handbook.

Read the following passage and the information about its source. Then decide whether each student sample is plagiarized or uses the source correctly. If the student sample is plagiarized, write "plagiarized"; if the sample is acceptable, write "OK."

ORIGINAL SOURCE

Our four friends [in *The Wizard of Oz*] finally gain entry to the Wizard's palace because Dorothy's tears of frustration undam a quite alarming reservoir of liquid in the guard. His face is quickly sodden with tears, and, watching this extreme performance, you are struck by the sheer number of occasions on which people cry in this film. Besides Dorothy and the guard, there is the Cowardly Lion, who bawls when Dorothy bops him on the nose; the Tin Man, who almost rusts up again from weeping; and Dorothy again, while she is in the clutches of the Witch. It occurs to you that if the hydrophobic Witch could only have been closer at hand on one of these occasions the movie might have been much shorter.

From Rushdie, Salman. "Out of Kansas: *The Wizard of Oz*." *Writers at the Movies: Twenty-Six Contemporary Authors Celebrate Twenty-Six Memorable Movies*, edited by Jim Shepard, HarperCollins, 2000, pp. 201-26. [The source passage is from pages 223-24. Page 224 begins with the words *been closer at hand*.]

1. The sheer number of occasions on which people cry in *The Wizard of Oz* is astounding.

2. Rushdie notes that so many characters cry in *The Wizard of Oz* that it's surprising the Wicked Witch did not get wet and melt away earlier in the film (223-24).

3. Rushdie points out the number of characters who weep in *The Wizard of Oz*: Dorothy cries tears of frustration before being allowed to enter the Wizard's palace, the guard at the palace becomes sodden with tears, the Cowardly Lion cries when Dorothy hits him on the nose, the Tin Man nearly rusts up again from crying, and Dorothy cries again when captured by the Witch (223).

4. Pointing out how many times characters cry in *The Wizard of Oz*, Rushdie observes that "if the hydrophobic Witch could only have been closer at hand on one of these occasions the movie might have been much shorter" (223-24).

5. Rushdie notes that Dorothy's weeping makes other characters cry, as when her tears "undam a quite alarming reservoir of liquid" from the guard in an extreme performance outside the Wizard's palace (223).

Avoiding plagiarism in MLA papers 5

For help with this exercise, see the section on avoiding plagiarism in MLA papers in your handbook.

Read the following passage and the information about its source. Then decide whether each student sample is plagiarized or uses the source correctly. If the student sample is plagiarized, write "plagiarized"; if the sample is acceptable, write "OK."

ORIGINAL SOURCE

The conversations in the [James Fenimore] Cooper books have a curious sound in our modern ears. To believe that such talk really ever came out of people's mouths would be to believe that there was a time when time was of no value to a person who thought he had something to say; when it was the custom to spread a two-minute remark out to ten; when a man's mouth was a rolling-mill, and busied itself all day long in turning four-foot pigs of thought into thirty-foot bars of conversational railroad iron by attenuation; when subjects were seldom faithfully stuck to, but the talk wandered all around and arrived nowhere; when conversations consisted mainly of irrelevancies, with here and there a relevancy, a relevancy with an embarrassed look, as not being able to explain how it got there.

From Twain, Mark. "Fenimore Cooper's Literary Offenses." *Selected Shorter Writings of Mark Twain*, edited by Walter Blair, Houghton Mifflin, 1962, pp. 227-38. [The source passage is from page 236.]

1. Mark Twain notes that readers of James Fenimore Cooper are required "to believe that there was a time when time was of no value to a person who thought he had something to say" (236).

2. Mark Twain wonders if people ever conversed the way Cooper's characters do and if people really did have all the time in the world to listen to one another's ramblings (236).

3. Among Mark Twain's objections to Cooper's writing is the rambling conversational style of his characters, who seldom stick faithfully to their subjects but allow their talk to wander all around and end up nowhere (236).

4. James Fenimore Cooper's dialogue consists mainly of irrelevancies, with an occasional embarrassed-looking relevancy that can't explain how it got there.

5. Mark Twain ridicules the dialogue in Cooper's novels as sounding peculiar to modern ears; he points out that the conversations wandered all around and arrived nowhere (236).

Hacker/Sommers, *Working with Sources: Exercises for Hacker Handbooks* (Boston: Bedford, 2018)

Recognizing common knowledge in MLA papers

For help with this exercise, see the section on recognizing common knowledge in MLA papers in your handbook.

Read each student passage and determine whether the student needs to cite the source of the information in an MLA paper. If the material does not need citation because it is common knowledge, write "common knowledge." If the material is not common knowledge and the student should cite the source, write "needs citation."

EXAMPLE

The playwright August Wilson won two Pulitzer Prizes in drama. *Common knowledge*
[Winners of well-known prizes such as the Pulitzer Prize are common knowledge because the information is readily available in any number of sources.]

1. Many of William Faulkner's novels are set in Yoknapatawpha County, a fictional part of Mississippi.

2. William Faulkner may have gotten the word *Yoknapatawpha* from a 1915 dictionary of the Choctaw language.

3. The writer and folklorist Zora Neale Hurston died in poverty in 1960.

4. William Shakespeare was the only playwright of his generation known to have a long-standing relationship with a single theater company.

5. Walt Disney fired and blacklisted all of his animators who went on strike in 1941.

6. William Wordsworth and Percy Bysshe Shelley were poets of the Romantic era.

7. As of 2012, the film *Titanic* had earned more than two billion dollars in box office revenue worldwide.

8. Heroic couplets are rhyming pairs of lines written in iambic pentameter.

9. Iris Murdoch wrote many sophisticated and complex novels before she succumbed to Alzheimer's disease.

10. George Lucas made a larger fortune by selling *Star Wars* toys than he made by selling tickets to *Star Wars*.

Integrating sources in MLA papers 1

For help with this exercise, see the section on integrating sources in MLA papers in your handbook.

Read the following passage and the information about its source. Then decide whether each student sample uses the source correctly. If the student has made an error in using the source, revise the sample to avoid the error. If the student has quoted correctly, write "OK."

ORIGINAL SOURCE

> In a work so elusive and kaleidoscopic, a number of perspectives suggest themselves. One is seeing the Ninth [Symphony] in light of its sister work, the *Missa Solemnis*. At the end of Beethoven's Mass the chorus is declaiming "*Dona nobis pacem*," the concluding prayer for peace, when the music is interrupted by the drums and trumpets of war. Just before the choir sings its last entreaty, the drums are still rolling in the distance. The Mass ends, then, with an unanswered prayer.
>
> Beethoven's answer to that prayer is the Ninth Symphony, where hope and peace are not demanded of the heavens. . . . In the end, though, the symphony presents us as many questions as answers, and its vision of utopia is proclaimed, not attained. What can be said with some certainty is that its position in the world is probably what Beethoven wanted it to be. In an unprecedented way for a composer, he stepped into history with a great ceremonial work that doesn't simply preach a sermon about freedom and brotherhood, but aspires to help bring them to pass. Partly because of its enigmas, so many ideologies have claimed the music for their own; over two centuries Communists, Christians, Nazis, and humanists have joined in the chorus. Leonard Bernstein conducted the Ninth at the celebration of the fall of the Berlin Wall, and what else would do the job? Now the Joy theme is the anthem of the European Union, a symbol of nations joining together. If you're looking for the universal, here it is.

> From Swafford, Jan. "Ludwig van Beethoven (1770-1827), Symphony No. 9 in D minor, Opus 125." *Boston Symphony Orchestra*, 3 May 2012, bso.http.internapcdn.net/bso/images/program_notes/beethoven_symphony9.pdf.

1. According to Swafford, Beethoven's Ninth Symphony is an answer to Beethoven's Mass, the *Missa Solemnis*, in which the chorus is singing "the concluding prayer for peace, when the music is interrupted by the drums of war."

2. Beethoven's *Missa Solemnis* ends with an interrupted prayer for peace, and his Ninth Symphony steps in to answer that prayer.

3. Swafford calls Beethoven's Ninth Symphony "elusive and kaleidoscopic," pointing out that it provides a "vision of utopia [that] is proclaimed, not attained."

4. One commentator has written that the Ninth Symphony "doesn't simply preach a sermon about freedom and brotherhood, but aspires to help bring them to pass" (Swafford).

5. The universal appeal of the Ninth Symphony is undeniable: groups as ideologically different as "Communists, Christians, Nazis, and humanists" have all "claimed the music for their own."

Hacker/Sommers, *Working with Sources: Exercises for Hacker Handbooks* (Boston: Bedford, 2018)

Integrating sources in MLA papers 2

For help with this exercise, see the section on integrating sources in MLA papers in your handbook.

Read the following passage and the information about its source. Then decide whether each student sample uses the source correctly. If the student has made an error in using the source, revise the sample to avoid the error. If the student has quoted correctly, write "OK."

ORIGINAL SOURCE

In 1827 two brothers from Switzerland named Giovanni and Pietro Del-Monico—the one a wine importer, the other a pastry chef—opened a shop on William Street [in New York City] with a half-dozen pine tables where customers could sample fine French pastries, coffee, chocolate, wine, and liquor. Three years later, the Delmonicos (as John and Peter now called themselves) opened a "Restaurant Français" next door that was among the first in town to let diners order from a menu of choices, at any time they pleased, and sit at their own cloth-covered tables. This was a sharp break from the fixed fare and simultaneous seatings at common hotel tables—so crowded (one guidebook warned) that your elbows were "pinned down to your sides like the wings of a trussed fowl." New Yorkers were a bit unsure about fancy foreign customs at first, and the earliest patrons tended to be resident European agents of export houses, who felt themselves marooned among a people with barbarous eating habits. The idea soon caught on, however; more restaurants appeared, and harried businessmen abandoned the ancient practice of going home for lunch.

From Burrows, Edwin G., and Mike Wallace. *Gotham: A History of New York City to 1898.* Oxford UP, 1999. [The source passage is from pages 436-37. Page 436 ends after the first dash in the first sentence.]

1. The Delmonico brothers' French restaurant was among the first eating establishments to let diners order from a menu of choices, at any time they pleased, and sit at their own cloth-covered tables (437).

2. As Edwin G. Burrows and Mike Wallace point out, restaurant culture in New York City changed forever with the arrival of the Delmonico brothers' French restaurant, which was among the first eating establishments "to let diners order from a menu of choices, at any time they pleased, and sit at their own cloth-covered tables" (437).

3. In their history of New York City's early years, Edwin G. Burrows and Mike Wallace describe the Delmonico brothers' first eating establishment, opened in 1827, as a shop consisting of "a half-dozen pine tables where customers could sample fine French pastries, coffee, chocolate, wine, and liquor" (437).

4. In 1830, the Delmonico brothers opened one of the first restaurants in New York City. "This was a sharp break from the fixed fare and simultaneous seatings at common hotel tables—so crowded (one guidebook warned) that your elbows were 'pinned down to your sides like the wings of a trussed fowl'" (Burrows and Wallace 437).

5. According to Burrows and Wallace, the Delmonico brothers' original shop enticed New Yorkers "with a half-dozen tables at which patrons could sample French pastries, coffee, chocolate, wine, and liquor" (437).

6. As Burrows and Wallace note, New Yorkers in 1830 felt "a bit unsure about [such] fancy foreign customs" as eating in a restaurant that offered a menu and separate tables (437).

7. Burrows and Wallace observe that the Delmonico brothers' restaurant first attracted resident European agents of export houses, who felt themselves marooned among a people with barbarous eating habits (437).

8. The Delmonico brothers' restaurant first attracted "resident European agents of export houses, who felt themselves marooned among a people with barbarous eating habits" (437).

9. According to Burrows and Wallace, "The idea [of a restaurant] soon caught on . . . and harried businessmen abandoned the ancient practice of going home for lunch" (437).

10. Native New Yorkers were at first suspicious of the concept of a restaurant. "The idea soon caught on, however; more restaurants appeared, and harried businessmen abandoned the ancient practice of going home for lunch" (437).

Hacker/Sommers, *Working with Sources: Exercises for Hacker Handbooks* (Boston: Bedford, 2018)

Integrating sources in MLA papers 3

For help with this exercise, see the section on integrating sources in MLA papers in your handbook.

Read the following passage and the information about its source. Then decide whether each student sample uses the source correctly. If the student has made an error in using the source, revise the sample to avoid the error. If the student has quoted correctly, write "OK."

ORIGINAL SOURCE

More than 1% of California's electricity comes from the wind. During breezy early mornings in summer, the contribution goes even higher. "At those times, the wind accounts for up to 8% of our electrical load," said Mary A. Ilyin, a wind researcher for Pacific Gas & Electric, the country's largest utility and a major booster of wind power.

Half of California's turbines . . . are located in Altamont Pass and feed directly into PG&E's grid. Most of the rest are found in two other major wind centers: Tehachapi Pass on the edge of the Mojave Desert between Bakersfield and Barstow, with a capacity of 458 megawatts, and San Gorgonio Pass north of Palm Springs (231 megawatts). Both are hooked up to the power lines of Southern California Edison.

From Golden, Frederic. "Electric Wind." *Los Angeles Times*, 24 Dec. 1990, p. B1.

1. Wind power accounts for more than 1% of California's electricity, reports Frederic Golden, and during breezy early mornings in summer, the contribution goes even higher (B1).

2. According to Frederic Golden, wind power accounts for more than 1% of California's electricity, and on breezy days "the contribution goes even higher" (B1).

3. Mary A. Ilyin reports that "wind energy accounts for as much as 8% of California's electricity" (qtd. in Golden B1).

4. On breezy summer mornings, says wind researcher Mary A. Ilyin, "the wind accounts for up to 8% of our [California's] electrical load" (qtd. in Golden B1).

5. California has pioneered the use of wind power. "Half of California's turbines . . . are located in Altamont Pass" (Golden B1).

Integrating sources in MLA papers 4

For help with this exercise, see the section on integrating sources in MLA papers in your handbook.

Read the following passage and the information about its source. Then decide whether each student sample uses the source correctly. If the student has made an error in using the source, revise the sample to avoid the error. If the student has quoted correctly, write "OK."

ORIGINAL SOURCE

Most of us think that S.U.V.s are much safer than sports cars. If you asked the young parents of America whether they would rather strap their infant child in the back seat of the TrailBlazer [a Chevrolet SUV] or the passenger seat of the Boxster [a Porsche sports car], they would choose the TrailBlazer. We feel that way because in the TrailBlazer our chances of surviving a collision with a hypothetical tractor-trailer in the other lane are greater than they are in the Porsche. What we forget, though, is that in the TrailBlazer you're also much more likely to hit the tractor-trailer because you can't get out of the way in time. In the parlance of the automobile world, the TrailBlazer is better at "passive safety." The Boxster is better when it comes to "active safety," which is every bit as important.

From Gladwell, Malcolm. "Big and Bad." *The New Yorker*, 12 Jan. 2004, pp. 28-33.
[The source passage is from page 31.]

1. Malcolm Gladwell points out that drivers feel safer in an SUV than in a sports car because they think that the SUV driver's "chances of surviving a collision with a hypothetical tractor-trailer in the other lane are greater" (31).

2. Gladwell argues that "active safety is every bit as important" as a vehicle's ability to withstand a collision (31).

3. A majority of drivers can, indeed, be wrong. "Most of us think that S.U.V.s are much safer than sports cars" (Gladwell 31).

4. According to Gladwell, American SUVs are more likely to be involved in collisions than other vehicles "because [they] can't get out of the way in time" (31).

5. Gladwell explains that most people expect an SUV "to survive a collision with a hypothetical tractor-trailer in the other lane" (31).

Hacker/Sommers, *Working with Sources: Exercises for Hacker Handbooks* (Boston: Bedford, 2018)

MLA documentation: in-text citations 1

For help with this exercise, see the MLA in-text citations section in your handbook.

Circle the letter of the MLA in-text citation that is handled correctly.

EXAMPLE

The student is quoting from pages 26-27 of the following source:

Follman, Mark. "Trigger Warnings." *Mother Jones*, Nov./Dec. 2015, pp. 22-29.

a. Mass shootings in America took a turn with Columbine; Follman argues that the teen shooters "authored a compelling new script at the dawn of the Internet age" (26-27).

b. Mass shootings in America took a turn with Columbine; Follman argues that the teen shooters "authored a compelling new script at the dawn of the Internet age" (pp. 26-27).

1. The student is quoting Christina Hoff Sommers from page 17 of the following book:

    Winegarner, Beth. *The Columbine Effect: How Five Teen Pastimes Got Caught in the Crossfire*. Lulu Press, 2013.

    a. In the wake of Columbine, according to Christina Hoff Sommers, "It has become fashionable to attribute pathology to millions of healthy male children" (qtd. in Winegarner 17).

    b. In the wake of Columbine, according to Christina Hoff Sommers, "It has become fashionable to attribute pathology to millions of healthy male children" (17).

2. The student is citing a blog post that appeared on the *Psychology Today* website:

    Ramsland, Katherine. "Mass Murder Motives." *Psychology Today*, 20 July 2012, www.psychologytoday.com/blog/shadow-boxing/201207/mass-murder-motives.

    a. Katherine Ramsland describes motives for mass murder that "rang[e] from revenge to despair to free-floating rage at the world" ("Mass").

    b. Katherine Ramsland describes motives for mass murder that "rang[e] from revenge to despair to free-floating rage at the world."

3. The student is quoting from page 472 of a scholarly article by Dianne T. Gereluk, Kent Donlevy, and Merlin B. Thompson.

    a. Gereluk, Donlevy, and Thompson have called the teacher's threat assessment role "onerous" and have expressed concern about the "tremendous burden of watching for potential threats" in and out of the classroom (472).

    b. Gereluk et al. have called the teacher's threat assessment role "onerous" and have expressed concern about the "tremendous burden of watching for potential threats" in and out of the classroom (472).

4. The student is using statistics from the following article:

   Follman, Mark. "Trigger Warnings." *Mother Jones*, Nov./Dec. 2015, pp. 22-29.

   a. In the seventy-two known Columbine copycat cases, 53% of the planned attacks involved guns, and 18% involved bombs or explosives (Follman 27).

   b. In the seventy-two known Columbine copycat cases, 53% of the planned attacks involved guns, and 18% involved bombs or explosives.

5. The student is summarizing information gathered from a map found in this source:

   Mosendz, Polly. "Map: Every School Shooting in America since 2013." *Newsweek*, 16 Oct. 2015, www.newsweek.com/list-school-shootings-america-2013-380535.

   a. An analysis of the map reveals that there is no regional concentration in the occurrence of school shootings. They happen everywhere in America ("Map").

   b. An analysis of the map reveals that there is no regional concentration in the occurrence of school shootings. They happen everywhere in America (Mosendz).

6. The student is quoting the author's exact words from this online video:

   Gladwell, Malcolm. "Malcolm Gladwell Discusses School Shootings." *YouTube*, 5 Oct. 2015, www.youtube.com/watch?v=27aWHudLmgs.

   a. Gladwell's assessment of the recent history of school shootings is eye-opening: "It's an overwhelmingly American phenomenon," he says.

   b. Gladwell's assessment of the recent history of school shootings is eye-opening: It's an overwhelmingly American phenomenon, he says.

7. The student is summarizing the following unsigned source:

   "Another Day, Another Tragic School Shooting." *The Washington Post*, 9 Oct. 2015, www.washingtonpost.com/opinions/another-day-another-tragic-school -shooting/2015/10/09/62f5077c-6eb5-11e5-b31c-d80d62b53e28_story.html. Editorial.

   a. Mental health treatment and peer counseling are good first steps to reducing school violence; restricting access to guns, however, is the most important step (Editorial).

   b. Mental health treatment and peer counseling are good first steps to reducing school violence; restricting access to guns, however, is the most important step ("Another").

8. The student is quoting from page 45 of the following source:

   Klein, Jessie. *The Bully Society: School Shootings and the Crisis of Bullying in America's Schools*. New York UP, 2013.

Hacker/Sommers, *Working with Sources: Exercises for Hacker Handbooks* (Boston: Bedford, 2018)

The list of works cited includes two works by Klein.

a. Klein, a sociology professor, raises the idea that "boys are pressured to behave in a host of essentially superhuman or nonhuman ways" (*Bully* 45).

b. Klein, a sociology professor, raises the idea that "boys are pressured to behave in a host of essentially superhuman or nonhuman ways" (45).

9. The student is paraphrasing from this short work from a website:

    "Effects of Bullying." *StopBullying.gov*, US Department of Health and Human Services, www.stopbullying.gov/at-risk/effects/. Accessed 5 Apr. 2016.

a. Violence against others can be a response to being chronically bullied. There is evidence that many school shooters and mass shooters have experienced bullying (US Department of Health and Human Services).

b. Violence against others can be a response to being chronically bullied. There is evidence that many school shooters and mass shooters have experienced bullying ("Effects").

10. The student quotes from a blog post:

    Brucculieri, Julia, and Cole Delbyck. "These Classic TV Episodes about School Shootings Are More Relevant Than Ever." *Huffington Post*, 24 Jan. 2016, www.huffingtonpost.com/entry/school-shootings-on-tv _us_56a14986e4b076aadcc5c94b?utm_hp_ref=school-shooting.

a. *Huffington Post* entertainment bloggers posted that a 2013 episode of *Glee* led some viewers to "[draw] connections between autism and Newtown, Connecticut shooter Adam Lanza" and the show's Becky character (Brucculieri and Delbyck).

b. *Huffington Post* entertainment bloggers posted that a 2013 episode of *Glee* led some viewers to "[draw] connections between autism and Newtown, Connecticut shooter Adam Lanza" and the show's Becky character (Brucculieri).

MLA documentation: in-text citations 2

For help with this exercise, see the MLA in-text citations section in your handbook.

Circle the letter of the MLA in-text citation that is handled correctly.

EXAMPLE

The student is quoting from page 148 of the following magazine article:

Als, Hilton. "Wayward Girl." *The New Yorker*, 18-25 Aug. 2003, pp. 147-49.

(a.) Als describes Cat Power as "a storyteller . . . [who] cares more about how she says something than about what she says" (148).

b. Als describes Cat Power as "a storyteller . . . [who] cares more about how she says something than about what she says." (148).

1. The student has used two sources by Nat Hentoff in the paper and is quoting from page 12 of the first source:

   Hentoff, Nat. *At the Jazz Band Ball: Sixty Years on the Jazz Scene*. U of California P, 2010.

   ---. *Listen to the Stories: Nat Hentoff on Jazz and Country Music*. HarperCollins Publishers, 1995.

   a. Hentoff notes that when Artie Shaw first quit playing jazz in 1939, Shaw "wanted to resign from the planet, not just music. It stopped being fun with success," a sentiment echoed by musicians such as Kurt Cobain decades later (12).

   b. Hentoff notes that when Artie Shaw first quit playing jazz in 1939, Shaw "wanted to resign from the planet, not just music. It stopped being fun with success," a sentiment echoed by musicians such as Kurt Cobain decades later (*At* 12).

2. The student is quoting from page 339 of the following book:

   Kerman, Joseph, and Gary Tomlinson. *Listen*. 7th ed., Bedford/St. Martin's, 2012.

   a. Though most composers in the early twentieth century were influenced by modernism, Kerman and Tomlinson note that some composers "kept on mining the reliable quarries of Romanticism for their own private veins of (they hoped) musical gold" (339).

   b. Though most composers in the early twentieth century were influenced by modernism, Kerman notes that some composers "kept on mining the reliable quarries of Romanticism for their own private veins of (they hoped) musical gold" (339).

3. The student is summarizing two magazine articles:

> Gates, David. "Report from a City of Ruins." Review of *The Rising*, by Bruce Springsteen. *Newsweek*, 29 July 2002, p. 56.

> Santoro, Gene. "Hey, He's Bruce." *The Nation*, 16 Sept. 2002, pp. 32-34.

a. In his album *The Rising*, Bruce Springsteen elevates his typical working-class subjects to the status of heroes in the post-September 11 world (Gates; Santoro).

b. In his album *The Rising*, Bruce Springsteen elevates his typical working-class subjects to the status of heroes in the post-September 11 world (Gates and Santoro).

4. The student is quoting from the following online review:

> Berman, Stuart. "The Flaming Lips: *The Terror*." *Pitchfork*, 4 Apr. 2013, www.pitchfork .com/reviews/albums/17804-the-flaming-lips-the-terror.

a. *Pitchfork* reviewer Stuart Berman explains that *The Terror* is an answer to the Flaming Lips' previous album, *Embryonic*; however, while "*Embryonic* played on themes of environmental destruction, *The Terror* deals in more personal turmoil — loneliness, depression, anxiety."

b. *Pitchfork* reviewer Stuart Berman explains that *The Terror* is an answer to the Flaming Lips' previous album, *Embryonic*; however, while "*Embryonic* played on themes of environmental destruction, *The Terror* deals in more personal turmoil — loneliness, depression, anxiety" ("Flaming").

5. The student is quoting from page 623 of the following selection in an anthology (a collection):

> Bangs, Lester. "Where Were You When Elvis Died?" *Rock and Roll Is Here to Stay*, edited by William McKeen, W. W. Norton, 2000, pp. 623-27.

a. Some might see Elvis Presley not "as a tragic figure . . . [but] more like the Pentagon, a giant armored institution nobody knows anything about except that its power is legendary" (Bangs and McKeen 623).

b. Some might see Elvis Presley not "as a tragic figure . . . [but] more like the Pentagon, a giant armored institution nobody knows anything about except that its power is legendary" (Bangs 623).

6. The student is quoting from page 42 of the following essay:

> Grigoriadis, Vanessa. "Growing Up Gaga." *Best Music Writing 2011*, edited by Alex Ross, Da Capo Press, 2011, pp. 34-52.

a. Wendy Starland, who introduced Lady Gaga to producer Rob Fisari, has said that Lady Gaga's "presence is enormous. And fearless" (Grigoriadis 42).

b. Wendy Starland, who introduced Lady Gaga to producer Rob Fisari, has said that Lady Gaga's "presence is enormous. And fearless" (qtd. in Grigoriadis 42).

Hacker/Sommers, *Working with Sources: Exercises for Hacker Handbooks* (Boston: Bedford, 2018)

7. The student is quoting from page E5 of the following newspaper article:

> Ratliff, Ben. "A Hall with Jazz on Its Mind: Basing a Season on Performers and New Works." *The New York Times*, 12 May 2004, pp. E1+.

a. Ratliff notes that Lincoln Center's jazz concerts have been held at Alice Tully Hall and Avery Fisher Hall, "respectable cultural landmarks that are nevertheless physically hostile to the sound of jazz percussion" (E5).

b. Ratliff notes that Lincoln Center's jazz concerts have been held at Alice Tully Hall and Avery Fisher Hall, "respectable cultural landmarks that are nevertheless physically hostile to the sound of jazz percussion" (E1+).

8. The student is paraphrasing from the following online article:

> Andrews, Travis M. "Hip-Hop Goes for Gay Marriage." *Salon*, 2 Apr. 2013, www.salon .com/2013/04/02/hip_hop_goes_for_gay_marriage.

a. Hip-hop scholars suggest that rappers' growing support for same-sex marriage mirrors society's changing values; of course, this transition is complicated by a history of homophobic lyrics (Andrews).

b. Hip-hop scholars suggest that rappers' growing support for same-sex marriage mirrors society's changing values; of course, this transition is complicated by a history of homophobic lyrics ("Hip-Hop").

9. The student is quoting from page 12 of the following magazine article:

> "U2's Spiritual Journey Defies Categorizing." *Christian Century*, 13 Feb. 2002, pp. 12-13.

a. While U2's music is infused with religious imagery and explicitly embraces Christian themes, the band's hard-living lifestyle makes "some pietistic Christians . . . question the band's beliefs" (*Christian Century* 12).

b. While U2's music is infused with religious imagery and explicitly embraces Christian themes, the band's hard-living lifestyle makes "some pietistic Christians . . . question the band's beliefs" ("U2's" 12).

10. The student is quoting from and paraphrasing the following online wiki entry:

> "Riot Grrrl." *Wikipedia*, 2004, www.en.wikipedia.org/wiki/Riot_grrrl.

a. *Wikipedia* notes that the term *riot grrrl* "became an almost meaningless media catchphrase" that was rarely used by artists themselves (Anonymous).

b. *Wikipedia* notes that the term *riot grrrl* "became an almost meaningless media catchphrase" that was rarely used by artists themselves ("Riot").

MLA documentation: in-text citations 3

For help with this exercise, see the MLA in-text citations section in your handbook.

Circle the letter of the MLA in-text citation that is handled correctly.

EXAMPLE

The student is quoting from page 187 of the following essay:

Pérez-Torres, Rafael. "Between Presence and Absence: *Beloved*, Postmodernism, and Blackness." *Toni Morrison's* Beloved*: A Casebook*, edited by William L. Andrews and Nellie Y. McKay, Oxford UP, 1999, pp. 179-201.

a. Amy describes the scars on Sethe's back as a tree, which, as suggested by Rafael Pérez-Torres, transforms "the signs of slavery . . . into an image of fruition instead of oppression." (187)

b. Amy describes the scars on Sethe's back as a tree, which, as suggested by Rafael Pérez-Torres, transforms "the signs of slavery . . . into an image of fruition instead of oppression" (187).

1. The student is quoting from page 195 of the following essay:

   Pérez-Torres, Rafael. "Between Presence and Absence: *Beloved*, Postmodernism, and Blackness." *Toni Morrison's* Beloved*: A Casebook*, edited by William L. Andrews and Nellie Y. McKay, Oxford UP, 1999, pp. 179-201.

   a. According to Pérez-Torres, *Beloved* "offers a radical revisioning and recounting of history" (195).

   b. According to Pérez-Torres, *Beloved* "offers a radical revisioning and recounting of history" ("Between" 195).

2. The student is quoting from page 183 of the following collection:

   Twain, Mark. *Adventures of Huckleberry Finn*. 1885. Edited by Gregg Camfield, Bedford/ St. Martin's, 2008. Bedford College Editions.

   a. As the novel progresses and he gets to know Jim better, Huck begins to understand that a black slave can experience emotions too. After observing Jim's mourning for the family he left behind, Huck says, "I do believe [Jim] cared just as much for his people as white folks does for their'n" (Twain 183).

   b. As the novel progresses and he gets to know Jim better, Huck begins to understand that a black slave can experience emotions too. After observing Jim's mourning for the family he left behind, Huck says, "I do believe [Jim] cared just as much for his people as white folks does for their'n" (Camfield 183).

3. The student is quoting from page 52 of the following book:

> Morrison, Toni. *Playing in the Dark: Whiteness and the Literary Imagination*. Vintage Books, 1993.

a. Morrison criticizes white authors for using black characters as mere props to expose their own characterizations:

> Africanism is the vehicle by which the American self knows itself as not enslaved, but free; not repulsive, but desirable; not helpless, but licensed and powerful; not historyless, but historical; not damned, but innocent; not a blind accident of evolution, but a progressive fulfillment of destiny. (52)

b. Morrison criticizes white authors for using black characters as mere props to expose their own characterizations:

> "Africanism is the vehicle by which the American self knows itself as not enslaved, but free; not repulsive, but desirable; not helpless, but licensed and powerful; not historyless, but historical; not damned, but innocent; not a blind accident of evolution, but a progressive fulfillment of destiny" (52).

4. The student is summarizing from page 32 of the following book:

> Morrison, Toni. *Beloved*. Plume, 1988.

The works cited list includes another work by Morrison.

a. Morrison deliberately alludes to Twain's book by sending Amy on a hunt for huckleberries when she first encounters Sethe in the woods (32).

b. Morrison deliberately alludes to Twain's book by sending Amy on a hunt for huckleberries when she first encounters Sethe in the woods (*Beloved* 32).

5. The student is quoting from page 339 of the following essay:

> Mayer, Sylvia. " 'You Like Huckleberries?' Toni Morrison's *Beloved* and Mark Twain's *Adventures of Huckleberry Finn*." *The Black Columbiad: Defining Moments in African American Literature and Culture*, edited by Werner Sollors and Maria Diedrich, Harvard UP, 1994, pp. 339-46. Harvard English Studies 19.

a. Mayer claims that Morrison uses the character of Amy "to explore . . . the conflict between 'freedom' and 'civilization' in a society deeply affected by slavery" (339).

b. Mayer claims that Morrison uses the character of Amy "to explore . . . the conflict between 'freedom' and 'civilization' in a society deeply affected by slavery" (Sollors and Diedrich 339).

Hacker/Sommers, *Working with Sources: Exercises for Hacker Handbooks* (Boston: Bedford, 2018)

6. The student is quoting from the following online source:

> Railton, Stephen. "Imaging 'Slavery' in MT's Books." *Mark Twain in His Times*, Stephen Railton/U of Virginia Library, 2012, twain.lib.virginia.edu/.

a. Railton suggests that, "even after slavery has been abolished, there remains the problem of understanding what it was like, what its legacy is, what it says about the nation's culture" ("Imaging").

b. Railton suggests that, "even after slavery has been abolished, there remains the problem of understanding what it was like, what its legacy is, what it says about the nation's culture."

7. The student is quoting from page 207 of the following article:

> Amare, Nicole, and Alan Manning. "Twain's *Huckleberry Finn*." *The Explicator*, vol. 62, no. 4, Summer 2004, pp. 206-09.

a. Some critics have asserted that Twain, like many authors of fiction, "relies heavily on names for satirical gain" (Amare and Manning 207).

b. Some critics have asserted that Twain, like many authors of fiction, "relies heavily on names for satirical gain" (Amare et al. 207).

8. The student is quoting from a book review accessed online:

> Atwood, Margaret. "Jaunted by Their Nightmares." Review of *Beloved*, by Toni Morrison. *The New York Times*, 13 Sept. 1987, nyti.ms/Y66IAB.

a. As *The New York Times* points out in its review, "Toni Morrison is careful not to make all the whites awful and all the blacks wonderful."

b. As Atwood points out in her review, "Toni Morrison is careful not to make all the whites awful and all the blacks wonderful."

9. The student is quoting Mark Twain from page 377 of the following article in a collection:

> Kaplan, Justin. "Born to Trouble: One Hundred Years of *Huckleberry Finn*." Adventures of Huckleberry Finn: *A Case Study in Critical Controversy*, edited by Gerald Graff and James Phelan, 2nd ed., Bedford/St. Martin's, 2004, pp. 371-81.

a. As Twain himself has said, *Huckleberry Finn* is a book in which "[a] sound heart and a deformed conscience come into collision and conscience suffers defeat" (qtd. in Kaplan 377).

b. As Twain himself has said, *Huckleberry Finn* is a book in which "[a] sound heart and a deformed conscience come into collision and conscience suffers defeat" (Kaplan 377).

10. The student is quoting from the following article accessed in an online database:

Hamlin, Annemarie, and Constance Joyner. "Racism and Real Life: *The Adventures of Huckleberry Finn* in the Undergraduate Survey of American Literature." *Radical Teacher*, vol. 80, 2007, pp. 12-18, www.mrsnewtonphs.com/uploads/8/7/7/4/8774500/racism_and_real_life.pdf.

a. Some critics argue that "students of Huck Finn can begin to see the social construction of race and its impact on blacks and whites through the novel's narrator, especially when the narrative is placed alongside something more contemporary like Morrison's work" (Hamlin and Joyner).

b. Some critics argue that "students of Huck Finn can begin to see the social construction of race and its impact on blacks and whites through the novel's narrator, especially when the narrative is placed alongside something more contemporary like Morrison's work" (Hamlin).

Hacker/Sommers, *Working with Sources: Exercises for Hacker Handbooks* (Boston: Bedford, 2018)

MLA documentation: identifying elements of sources

For help with this exercise, see the MLA identifying elements of sources section in your handbook.

Circle the letter of the correct answer for each question using information in the source provided.

SOURCE: A SHORT WORK FROM A WEBSITE

1. In your paper, you quote from the internal page of this site. How would you start a works cited entry for the internal page?

    a. Ahearn, Amy. "Willa Cather: A Brief Biographical Sketch."

    b. Jewell, Andrew, editor. *The Willa Cather Archive*.

2. What date would you use in a works cited entry for the internal page?

    a. 2017

    b. Jan. 2017

SOURCE: AN ARTICLE ACCESSED THROUGH A DATABASE

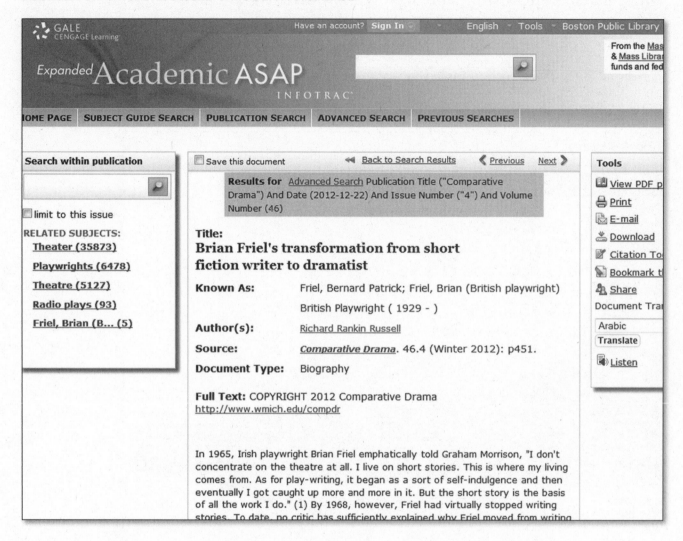

3. How would you cite the publication information for the journal article in this database record? (The article is more than one page long.)

   a. *Comparative Drama* 46.4 (2012), 451.

   b. *Comparative Drama*, vol. 46, no. 4, Winter 2012, pp. 451+.

4. How would you begin a works cited entry for this article?

   a. Russell, Richard Rankin.

   b. Friel, Bernard Patrick.

Hacker/Sommers, *Working with Sources: Exercises for Hacker Handbooks* (Boston: Bedford, 2018)

SOURCE: A PRINT BOOK

[Title page]

THE SECRET LIFE OF PRONOUNS

WHAT OUR WORDS SAY ABOUT US

James W. Pennebaker

BLOOMSBURY PRESS
New York   Berlin   London   Sydney

[Copyright page]

Copyright © 2011 by James W. Pennebaker

All rights reserved. No part of this book may be used or reproduced in
any manner whatsoever without written permission from the publisher
except in the case of brief quotations embodied in critical articles or reviews.
For information address Bloomsbury Press, 175 Fifth Avenue, New York, NY 10010.

Published by Bloomsbury Press, New York

All papers used by Bloomsbury Press are natural, recyclable products
made from wood grown in well-managed forests. The manufacturing
processes conform to the environmental regulations of the country of origin.

LIBRARY OF CONGRESS CATALOGING-IN-PUBLICATION DATA

Pennebaker, James W.
The secret life of pronouns : what our words say about us /
James W. Pennebaker. —1st U.S. ed.
p.   cm.
Includes bibliographical references and index.
ISBN: 978-1-60819-480-3
1. English language—Pronoun.   2. English language—Grammar.   I. Title.
PE1261.P46 2011
425'.55—dc22
2011001289

Copyright © 2011 by James W. Pennebaker

All rights reserved. No part of this book may be used or reproduced in
any manner whatsoever without written permission from the publisher
except in the case of brief quotations embodied in critical articles or reviews.
For information address Bloomsbury Press, 175 Fifth Avenue, New York, NY 10010.

Published by Bloomsbury Press, New York

---

5. How would you begin the works cited entry for this book?

  a. Pennebaker, James W. *THE SECRET LIFE OF PRONOUNS: WHAT OUR WORDS SAY ABOUT US.*

  b. Pennebaker, James W. *The Secret Life of Pronouns: What Our Words Say about Us.*

6. How would you cite the place of publication for this book in an MLA works cited entry?

  a. New York and Berlin:

  b. No place of publication is used for a book.

7. How would you end the MLA works cited entry for this book?

  a. Bloomsbury Press, 2011.

  b. Bloomsbury P, 2011.

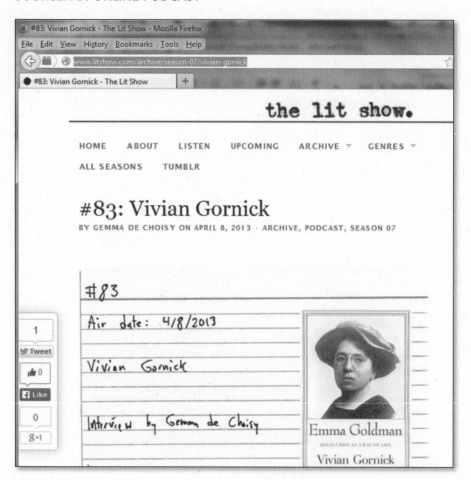

8. What is the correct works cited entry for this podcast, which is an interview with writer Vivian Gornick conducted by Gemma de Choisy? The podcast's website gives no sponsor. The URL for the podcast is http://www.litshow.com/archive/season-07/vivian-gornick, and your date of access was January 30, 2014.

a. "#83: Vivian Gornick." *The Lit Show*, 8 Apr. 2013, www.litshow.com/archive/season-07/vivian-gornick. Accessed 30 Jan. 2014.

b. Gornick, Vivian. "#83: Vivian Gornick." Interview by Gemma de Choisy. *The Lit Show*, 8 Apr. 2013, www.litshow.com/archive/season-07/vivian-gornick.

Hacker/Sommers, *Working with Sources: Exercises for Hacker Handbooks* (Boston: Bedford, 2018)

[Title page of anthology]

The Consumer Society Reader

EDITED BY JULIET B. SCHOR AND
DOUGLAS B. HOLT

THE NEW PRESS
NEW YORK

[First page of essay]

5
Jean Baudrillard
"THE IDEOLOGICAL GENESIS OF NEEDS"[1]
(1969)

The rapturous satisfactions of consumption surround us, clinging to objects as if to the sensory residues of the previous day in the delirious excursion of a dream. As to the logic that regulates this strange discourse—surely it compares to what Freud uncovered in *The Interpretation of Dreams*? But we have scarcely advanced beyond the explanatory level of naive psychology and the medieval dreambook. We believe in "Consumption": we believe in a real subject, motivated by needs and confronted by real objects as sources of satisfaction. It is a thoroughly vulgar metaphysic. And contemporary psychology, sociology and economic science are all complicit in the fiasco. So the time has come to deconstruct all the assumptive notions involved—object, need, aspiration, *consumption* itself—for it would make as little sense to theorize the quotidian from surface evidence as to interpret the manifest discourse of a dream: it is rather the dream-work and the dream-processes that must be analyzed in order to recover the unconscious logic of a more profound discourse. And it is the workings and processes of an unconscious social logic that must be retrieved beneath the consecrated ideology of consumption.

1. CONSUMPTION AS A LOGIC OF SIGNIFICATIONS

The empirical "object," given in its contingency of form, color, material, function and discourse (or, if it is a cultural object, in its aesthetic finality) is a myth. How often it has been wished away! But the object is *nothing*. It is nothing but the different types of relations and significations that converge, contradict themselves, and twist around it, as such—the hidden logic that not only arranges this bundle of relations, but directs the manifest discourse that overlays and occludes it.

THE LOGICAL STATUS OF OBJECTS

Insofar as I make use of a refrigerator as a machine, it is not an object. It is a refrigerator. Talking about refrigerators or automobiles in terms

---

9. You have used the essay on the right from the anthology whose title page is on the left. What information would come first in your MLA works cited entry?

   a. Schor, Juliet B., and Douglas B. Holt

   b. Baudrillard, Jean

10. What information shown on these two pages do you *not* need in an MLA works cited entry for the essay?

    a. Edited by Juliet B. Schor and Douglas B. Holt

    b. New York

MLA documentation: works cited 1

For help with this exercise, see the MLA works cited section in your handbook.

Circle the letter of the works cited entry that is handled correctly.

EXAMPLE

The student has quoted from "Facebook Hitman Highlights Organized Crime's Online Presence," by Miriam Wells, a short work on an unpaginated website, *InSight Crime*, sponsored by Open Society Foundations. The publication date is June 21, 2013, and the article is located at this URL: www.insightcrime.org/news-analysis/facebook-hitman-highlights-organized-crimes-online-presence.

(a.) Wells, Miriam. "Facebook Hitman Highlights Organized Crime's Online Presence." *InSight Crime*, Open Society Foundations, 21 June 2013, www.insightcrime.org/news-analysis/facebook-hitman-highlights-organized-crimes-online-presence.

b. Wells, Miriam. "Facebook Hitman Highlights Organized Crime's Online Presence." *InSight Crime*, 21 June 2013, www.insightcrime.org/news-analysis/facebook-hitman-highlights-organized-crimes-online-presence.

1. The student has quoted from James O. Finckenauer's article "Problems of Definition: What Is Organized Crime?" The student accessed this article on May 3, 2012, in the database *Springer Link* at the stable URL www.link.springer.com/journal/12117. The article appeared on pages 63-83 of the journal *Trends in Organized Crime*, volume 8, issue 3, published in March 2005.

   a. Finckenauer, James. "Problems of Definition: What Is Organized Crime?" *Trends in Organized Crime*, Mar. 2005, pp. 63-83. *Springer Link*, www.link.springer.com/journal/12117.

   b. Finckenauer, James. "Problems of Definition: What Is Organized Crime?" *Trends in Organized Crime*, vol. 8, no. 3, Mar. 2005, pp. 63-83. *Springer Link*, www.link.springer.com/journal/12117.

2. The student has quoted from page 759 of *The American Promise: A History of the United States*, 5th edition, written by James L. Roark, Michael P. Johnson, Patricia Cline Cohen, Sarah Stage, and Susan M. Hartmann and published in 2012 by Bedford/St. Martin's.

   a. Roark, James L., Michael P. Johnson, Patricia Cline Cohen, Sarah Stage, and Susan M. Hartmann. *The American Promise: A History of the United States*. 5th ed., Bedford/St. Martin's, 2012.

   b. Roark, James L., et al. *The American Promise: A History of the United States*. 5th ed., Bedford/St. Martin's, 2012.

3. The student has paraphrased from page 334 of the sixth edition of the book *Organized Crime in Our Times*, by Jay Albanese. The book was published by Routledge in 2015.

   a. Albanese, Jay. *Organized Crime in Our Times*. 6th ed., Routledge, 2015.

   b. Albanese, Jay. *Organized Crime in Our Times*. 6th ed., Routledge, 2015, p. 334.

4. The student has quoted dialogue from the 1972 film *The Godfather*, starring Marlon Brando and Al Pacino and directed by Francis Ford Coppola. The film was distributed by Paramount Pictures.

   a. *The Godfather*. Directed by Francis Ford Coppola, performances by Marlon Brando and Al Pacino, Paramount Pictures, 1972.

   b. Coppola, Francis Ford, director. *The Godfather*. Performances by Marlon Brando and Al Pacino, Paramount Pictures, 1972.

5. The student has quoted from Larry McShane's article "Mafia Files from Organized Crime Heyday Sell for More Than $10,000 at Auction," published on June 23, 2011, on the news site *nydailynews.com*, sponsored by NY Daily News and located at this web address: www.nydailynews.com/new-york/mafia-files-organized-crime-heyday-sell-10-000-auction-article-1.131313.

   a. McShane, Larry. "Mafia Files from Organized Crime Heyday Sell for More Than $10,000 at Auction." *nydailynews.com*, 23 June 2011, www.nydailynews.com/new-york/mafia-files-organized-crime-heyday-sell-10-000-auction-article-1.131313.

   b. McShane, Larry. "Mafia Files from Organized Crime Heyday Sell for More Than $10,000 at Auction." *nydailynews.com*, NY Daily News, 23 June 2011, www.nydailynews.com/new-york/mafia-files-organized-crime-heyday-sell-10-000-auction-article-1.131313.

6. The student has quoted from page 86 of Nicole Rafter and Michelle Brown's book *Criminology Goes to the Movies: Crime Theory and Popular Culture*, published by New York University Press in 2011.

   a. Rafter, Nicole, and Michelle Brown. *Criminology Goes to the Movies: Crime Theory and Popular Culture*. New York UP, 2011.

   b. Rafter, Nicole, and Michelle Brown. *Criminology Goes to the Movies: Crime Theory and Popular Culture*. New York University Press, 2011.

7. The student has summarized a review of *Drug War Zone: Frontline Dispatches from the Streets of El Paso and Juárez*, a book by Howard Campbell. The review, titled "The Murderers of Mexico," by Alma Guillermoprieto, appeared in the October 28, 2010, issue of *The New York Review of Books*. The writer accessed the article through the following URL: www.nybooks.com/articles/2010/10/28/murderers-mexico.

   a. Guillermoprieto, Alma. "The Murderers of Mexico." Review of *Drug War Zone: Frontline Dispatches from the Streets of El Paso and Juárez*, by Howard Campbell. *The New York Review of Books*, 28 Oct. 2010, www.nybooks.com/articles/2010/10/28/murderers-mexico.

   b. Guillermoprieto, Alma. "The Murderers of Mexico." *The New York Review of Books*, 28 Oct. 2010, www.nybooks.com/articles/2010/10/28/murderers-mexico.

Hacker/Sommers, *Working with Sources: Exercises for Hacker Handbooks* (Boston: Bedford, 2018)

8. The student has quoted from "*Gangster Squad* Whitewashes the LAPD's Criminal Past," in the online magazine *Salon* (www.salon.com/2013/01/10/gangster_squad_whitewashes _the_lapds_criminal_past). The article was written by Andrew O'Hehir and published on January 10, 2013.

   a. O'Hehir, Andrew. "*Gangster Squad* Whitewashes the LAPD's Criminal Past." *Salon*, 10 Jan. 2013, www.salon.com.

   b. O'Hehir, Andrew. "*Gangster Squad* Whitewashes the LAPD's Criminal Past." *Salon*, 10 Jan. 2013, www.salon.com/2013/01/10/gangster_squad_whitewashes_the_lapds_criminal_past.

9. The student has quoted from a March 10, 2003, *Wall Street Journal* article titled "Mobster Chic: It's Menswear a la 'Sopranos.'" The story was written by Teri Agins and Joe Flint and appeared on page B1.

   a. Agins, Teri, and Joe Flint. "Mobster Chic: It's Menswear a la 'Sopranos.'" *The Wall Street Journal*, March 10, 2003, p. B1.

   b. Agins, Teri, and Joe Flint. "Mobster Chic: It's Menswear a la 'Sopranos.'" *The Wall Street Journal*, 10 Mar. 2003, p. B1.

10. The student has quoted from an article titled "Violent Episode," published in *People* magazine on February 10, 2003. The article, for which no author is listed, appeared on page 126.

    a. "Violent Episode." *People*, 10 Feb. 2003, p. 126.

    b. Anonymous. "Violent Episode." *People*, 10 Feb. 2003, p. 126.

MLA documentation: works cited 2

For help with this exercise, see the MLA works cited section in your handbook.

Circle the letter of the works cited entry that is handled correctly.

EXAMPLE

The student has quoted from a book, *Understanding Indian Movies: Culture, Cognition, and Cinematic Imagination*, by Patrick Colm Hogan. It was published in 2008 by the University of Texas Press.

a. Hogan, Patrick Colm. *Understanding Indian Movies*. Austin: U of Texas P, 2008.

b. Hogan, Patrick Colm. *Understanding Indian Movies: Culture, Cognition, and Cinematic Imagination*. Austin: U of Texas P, 2008.

1. The student has cited a book, *Not Just Bollywood: Indian Directors Speak*, by Tula Goenka. The book was published by Om Books International in 2014.

   a. Goenka, Tula. *Not Just Bollywood: Indian Directors Speak*. Om Books International, 2014.

   b. Goenka, Tula. *Not Just Bollywood: Indian Directors Speak*. Om, 2014.

2. The student has cited the article "Kishore Kumar," by Sushama Shelly. It appeared on pages 95-96 of the November 2002 edition of the magazine *CinéBlitz*.

   a. Shelly, Sushama. "Kishore Kumar." *CinéBlitz*, Nov. 2002, pp. 95-96.

   b. Shelly, Sushama. "Kishore Kumar." *CinéBlitz*, November 2002, pp. 95-96.

3. The student has paraphrased material from the article "Playback Time: A Brief History of Bollywood 'Film Songs,'" by Nasreen Munni Kabir. It appeared on pages 41-43 of the May-June 2002 issue of the magazine *Film Comment*. The paper includes a citation of a book, *Bollywood: The Indian Cinema Story*, by the same author.

   a. Kabir, Nasreen Munni. "Playback Time: A Brief History of Bollywood 'Film Songs.'" *Film Comment*, May-June 2002, pp. 41-43.

   b. ---. "Playback Time: A Brief History of Bollywood 'Film Songs.'" *Film Comment*, May-June 2002, pp. 41-43.

4. The student has used a quotation from a January 2, 2015, article written by Maseeh Rahman titled "Bollywood Film Fans Fall in Love with PK despite Hindu Nationalist Protests." The article was found on a website titled *theguardian* at this URL: www.theguardian.com/film/2015/jan/02/bollywood-film-pk-hindu-nationalist-protests-india-aamir-khan.

   a. Maseeh Rahman. "Bollywood Film Fans Fall in Love with PK despite Hindu Nationalist Protests." *theguardian*, 2 Jan. 2015, www.theguardian.com/film/2015/jan/02/bollywood-film-pk-hindu-nationalist-protests-india-aamir-khan.

   b. Rahman, Maseeh. "Bollywood Film Fans Fall in Love with PK despite Hindu Nationalist Protests." *theguardian*, 2 Jan. 2015, www.theguardian.com/film/2015/jan/02/bollywood-film-pk-hindu-nationalist-protests-india-aamir-khan.

5. The student has quoted from a foreword by Tom Alter in a book, *Flashback: My Life and Times in Bollywood and Beyond*, by Bob Christo. The book was published by Penguin Books in 2011. The foreword appears on pages vii-viii.

   a. Alter, Tom. Foreword. *Flashback: My Life and Times in Bollywood and Beyond*, by Bob Christo, Penguin Books, 2011, pp. vii-viii.

   b. Christo, Bob. *Flashback: My Life and Times in Bollywood and Beyond*, foreword by Tom Alter, Penguin Books, 2011, pp. vii-viii.

6. The student has paraphrased material from an online video posted on a YouTube channel. The video, titled "Vijay Anand (Goldie Anand) Biography," was posted on May 16, 2013, at this web address: www.youtube.com/watch?v=9QUjqIZHkds.

   a. "Vijay Anand (Goldie Anand) Biography." *YouTube*, 16 May 2013, www.youtube.com.

   b. "Vijay Anand (Goldie Anand) Biography." *YouTube*, 16 May 2013, www.youtube.com/watch?v=9QUjqIZHkds.

7. The student has summarized material in a chapter titled "Hinduism" in the book *World Religions: A Historical Approach* by S. A. Nigosian. The student used the fourth edition of the book, which was published in 2008 by Bedford/St. Martin's. The chapter appears on pages 133-71.

   a. Nigosian, S. A. "Hinduism." *World Religions: A Historical Approach*, 4th ed., Bedford/St. Martin's, 2008, pp. 133-71.

   b. Nigosian, S. A. "Hinduism." *World Religions: A Historical Approach*, 4th ed., Bedford/St. Martin's, 2008.

8. The student has cited an article, "Fatwa Issued against 'Slumdog Millionaire' Composer A. R. Rahman," by Nyay Bhushan, which appeared on the website *The Hollywood Reporter*, sponsored by Hollywood Reporter. The article was published on September 12, 2015, at the URL www.hollywoodreporter.com/news/fatwa-issued-slumdog-millionaire-composer-822668.

   a. Bhushan, Nyay. "Fatwa Issued against 'Slumdog Millionaire' Composer." *The Hollywood Reporter*, Hollywood Reporter, 12 Sept. 2015, www.hollywoodreporter.com/news/fatwa-issued -slumdog-millionaire-composer-822668.

   b. Bhushan, Nyay. "Fatwa Issued against 'Slumdog Millionaire' Composer." *The Hollywood Reporter*, 12 Sept. 2015, www.hollywoodreporter.com/news/fatwa-issued-slumdog-millionaire -composer-822668.

9. The student has quoted dialogue from a film, *Dookudo*, directed by Sreenu Vaitla and starring Mahesh Babu and Samantha Ruth Prabhu. The film appeared on a DVD released in 2011 by Volga Videos.

   a. Vaitla, Sreenu, director. *Dookudo*. Volga Videos, 2011.

   b. *Dookudo*. Directed by Sreenu Vaitla, performances by Mahesh Babu and Samantha Ruth Prabhu, Volga Videos, 2011.

Hacker/Sommers, *Working with Sources: Exercises for Hacker Handbooks* (Boston: Bedford, 2018)

10. The student has quoted from "*Dookudo*, the Biggest Hit You've Never Heard Of," a review of the Indian film *Dookudo*, directed by Sreenu Vaitla. The review was written by Steven Zeitchik and published in the online version of the newspaper *Los Angeles Times* (latimesblogs.latimes .com/movies/2011/09/dookudu-daring-dashing-showtimes-reviews-prince-mahesh-samantha .html) on September 27, 2011.

a. Zeitchik, Steven. "*Dookudo*, the Biggest Hit You've Never Heard Of." Review of *Dookudo*, directed by Sreenu Vaitla. *Los Angeles Times*, 27 Sept. 2011, latimesblogs.latimes.com/movies/ 2011/09/dookudu-daring-dashing-showtimes-reviews-prince-mahesh-samantha.html.

b. Zeitchik, Steven. "*Dookudo*, the Biggest Hit You've Never Heard Of." *Los Angeles Times*, 27 Sept. 2011, latimesblogs.latimes.com/movies/2011/09/dookudu-daring-dashing-showtimes -reviews-prince-mahesh-samantha.html.

MLA documentation: works cited 3

For help with this exercise, see the MLA works cited section in your handbook.

Circle the letter of the works cited entry that is handled correctly.

EXAMPLE

The student has paraphrased information from the book *Breach of Faith: Hurricane Katrina and the Near Death of a Great American City*, by Jed Horne. The book was published in New York in 2008 by Random House.

a. Horne, Jed. *Breach of Faith: Hurricane Katrina and the Near Death of a Great American City.* New York, Random House, 2008.

b. Horne, Jed. *Breach of Faith: Hurricane Katrina and the Near Death of a Great American City.* Random House, 2008.

1. The student has quoted from an article about Hurricane Sandy in the January 2013 issue of *Runner's World*. The article, "The Storm [and Everything After]," which appeared on pages 68-69, has no author listed.

   a. Anonymous. "The Storm [and Everything After]." *Runner's World*, Jan. 2013, pp. 68-69.

   b. "The Storm [and Everything After]." *Runner's World*, Jan. 2013, pp. 68-69.

2. The student has quoted from an article titled "The Katrina Conspiracies: The Problem of Trust in Rebuilding an American City," which was published in volume 35, issue 2, of *Journal of Urban History* in January 2009. The article appeared on pages 207-19 and was accessed using the *Academic OneFile* database at the URL go.galegroup.com.ezproxy.bpl.org/. The authors of the article are Arnold R. Hirsch and Lee A. Levert.

   a. Hirsch, Arnold R., and Lee A. Levert. "The Katrina Conspiracies: The Problem of Trust in Rebuilding an American City." *Journal of Urban History*, volume 35, number 2, 2009, pp. 207-19.

   b. Hirsch, Arnold R., and Lee A. Levert. "The Katrina Conspiracies: The Problem of Trust in Rebuilding an American City." *Journal of Urban History*, vol. 35, no. 2, 2009, pp. 207-19. *Academic OneFile*, go.galegroup.com.ezproxy.bpl.org/.

3. The student has paraphrased information from an article titled "Hurricane Katrina as a Bureaucratic Nightmare," written by Vicki Bier. The article appeared on pages 243-54 of the anthology *On Risk and Disaster: Lessons from Hurricane Katrina*. The anthology was edited by Ronald J. Daniels, Donald F. Kettl, and Howard Kunreuther and was published in 2006 by the University of Pennsylvania Press.

   a. Bier, Vicki. "Hurricane Katrina as a Bureaucratic Nightmare." *On Risk and Disaster: Lessons from Hurricane Katrina*, edited by Ronald J. Daniels et al., U of Pennsylvania P, 2006, pp. 243-54.

   b. Daniels, Ronald J., et al., editors. *On Risk and Disaster: Lessons from Hurricane Katrina*. Vicki Bier, "Hurricane Katrina as a Bureaucratic Nightmare," U of Pennsylvania P, 2006, pp. 243-54.

4. The student has quoted information from a newspaper article that appeared in print on July 13, 2012, in *The Gardner News*. The article, written by Sam Bonacci and titled "Building Haiti Clinic Adds Up to Journey for Gardner Community," begins on page 1 and continues on page 4.

   a. Bonacci, Sam. "Building Haiti Clinic Adds Up to Journey for Gardner Community." *The Gardner News*, 13 July 2012, pp. 1, 4.

   b. Bonacci, Sam. "Building Haiti Clinic Adds Up to Journey for Gardner Community." *The Gardner News*, 13 July 2012, pp. 1+.

5. The student has paraphrased information from the article "How Weather Could Link Japan Radiation to US," which appeared on the *Scientific American* website (www.scientificamerican.com/article/weather-japan-radiation-united-states/) on March 16, 2011. The article was written by Jim Andrews and AccuWeather.

   a. Andrews, Jim, and AccuWeather. "How Weather Could Link Japan Radiation to US." *Scientific American*, 16 Mar. 2011, www.scientificamerican.com/article/weather-japan-radiation -united-states/.

   b. Andrews, Jim, and AccuWeather. "How Weather Could Link Japan Radiation to US." *Scientific American*, www.scientificamerican.com/article/weather-japan-radiation-united-states/.

6. The student has summarized information from a televised interview with Fareed Zakaria, conducted by Ali Velshi. Video from the interview, titled "Was Hurricane Sandy a Wake-Up Call?," was posted on the *Your Money* blog on the CNN website at the URL yourmoney .blogs.cnn.com/2012/11/23/was-hurricane-sandy-a-wake-up-call/?hpt=ym_bn2. The interview took place on November 21, 2012.

   a. Zakaria, Fareed. "Was Hurricane Sandy a Wake-Up Call?" Interview by Ali Velshi, *Your Money*, CNN, 21 Nov. 2012, yourmoney.blogs.cnn.com/2012/11/23/was-hurricane-sandy-a-wake -up-call/?hpt=ym_bn2.

   b. Velshi, Ali. "Was Hurricane Sandy a Wake-Up Call?" Interviewed Fareed Zakaria, *Your Money*, CNN, 21 Nov. 2012, yourmoney.blogs.cnn.com/2012/11/23/was-hurricane-sandy-a-wake -up-call/?hpt=ym_bn2.

7. The student has paraphrased information from a film on DVD titled *Japan's Killer Quake*, which was released by PBS in 2011. The film was narrated by Corey Johnson and directed by Rae Gilder and Tom Pearson.

   a. *Japan's Killer Quake*. Directed by Rae Gilder and Tom Pearson. Narr. Corey Johnson. PBS, 2011.

   b. *Japan's Killer Quake*. Directed by Rae Gilder and Tom Pearson, narrated by Corey Johnson, PBS, 2011.

Hacker/Sommers, *Working with Sources: Exercises for Hacker Handbooks* (Boston: Bedford, 2018)

8. The student has quoted from a document, *Navigating the Unknown: A Practical Lifeline for Decision-Makers in the Dark*, written by Patrick Lagadec and translated by Peter Leonard. The document was published by Crisis Response Journal in Thatcham, United Kingdom, in 2013.

   a. Lagadec, Patrick. *Navigating the Unknown: A Practical Lifeline for Decision-Makers in the Dark*. Translated by Peter Leonard, Crisis Response Journal, 2013.

   b. Lagadec, Patrick, and translated by Peter Leonard. *Navigating the Unknown: A Practical Lifeline for Decision-Makers in the Dark*, Crisis Response Journal, 2013.

9. The student has paraphrased a blog entry titled "Katrina," written by Chris Matthew Sciabarra on his blog, *Notablog*. The entry was posted at the URL www.nyu.edu/projects/sciabarra/notablog/archives/000727.html on September 6, 2005, and the student accessed it on February 2, 2009.

   a. Sciabarra, Chris Matthew. "Katrina." *Notablog*, 6 Sept. 2005, www.nyu.edu/projects/sciabarra/notablog/archives/000727.html.

   b. Sciabarra, Chris Matthew. "Katrina." *Notablog*, 6 Sept. 2005, www.nyu.edu/projects/sciabarra/notablog/archives/000727.html. Accessed 2 Feb. 2009.

10. The student has summarized information from an article on the web titled "Post-Katrina Education Problems Linger." The article appeared on the website *eSchool News* on August 30, 2007, at the URL http://www.eschoolnews.com/2007/08/30/post-katrina-education-problems-linger/. No author is given.

   a. "Post-Katrina Education Problems Linger." *eSchool News*, 30 Aug. 2007.

   b. "Post-Katrina Education Problems Linger." *eSchool News*, 30 Aug. 2007, www.eschoolnews.com/2007/08/30/post-katrina-education-problems-linger/.

MLA documentation

For help with this exercise, see the sections on MLA documentation in your handbook.

Write "true" if the statement is true or "false" if it is false.

1. A parenthetical citation in the text of a paper must always include a URL if the source is from the web.

2. The works cited list is organized alphabetically by authors' last names (or by title for a work with no author).

3. When in-text citations are used throughout a paper, there is no need for a works cited list at the end of the paper.

4. An in-text citation names the author (if there is an author) either in a signal phrase introducing the cited material or in parentheses after the cited material.

5. When a work's author is unknown, the work is listed under "Anonymous" in the list of works cited.

6. All authors are listed last name first, followed by first name, in the works cited list.

7. When a work has no page number, it is possible that nothing will appear in parentheses to mark the end of a citation.

8. In the parentheses marking the end of an in-text citation, the abbreviation "p." or "pp." is used before the page number(s).

9. When a paper cites two or more works by the same author, the in-text citation includes at least the author's name and the title (or a short version of the title).

10. For a works cited entry for a web source, a permalink (static, permanent link) or DOI (digital object identifier) is preferable to a URL.

Hacker/Sommers, *Working with Sources: Exercises for Hacker Handbooks* (Boston: Bedford, 2018)

Thesis statements in APA papers 1

For help with this exercise, see the section on thesis statements in APA papers in your handbook.

Circle the letter of the sentence in each pair that would work well as the thesis statement for a research paper from five to ten pages long. Remember that a thesis should be a central idea that requires supporting evidence; it should be of adequate scope for a five- to ten-page paper; and it should be sharply focused.

EXAMPLE

a. Believers in so-called alien abductions think that extraterrestrials have contacted humans, but a better explanation for such experiences is the phenomenon known as sleep paralysis.

b. At least several hundred Americans — and perhaps many more — believe that they have been attacked in their beds by extraterrestrial beings.

1. a. American women who expect motherhood to be completely fulfilling will be seriously disappointed when they encounter the many unpleasant realities of child care.

   b. Because American culture usually depicts mother-child relationships as unambiguously positive, women who feel ambivalent about the sacrifices of motherhood can suffer from a depressing sense of isolation.

2. a. Though collecting physiological data is important, an assessment that includes psychological, cultural, and even spiritual information will better equip a nurse to treat a client.

   b. Assessment is an important part of a nurse's role because it helps in treatment.

3. a. Research has demonstrated that showing an eyewitness sequential photographs of suspects rather than a lineup reduces mistaken identifications, but for a variety of reasons most police departments in the United States do not want to change their methods.

   b. Many people are jailed — and some are even executed — in the United States based solely on eyewitness testimony, which can sometimes be mistaken, but little has been done to correct the problem.

4. a. According to a 2013 study, 89% of American parents believe that violent video games negatively affect their children.

   b. Studies have not conclusively proved that violent video games cause aggressive behavior, but new longitudinal research may lead to more conclusive results.

5. a. Although adults often believe that children are emotionally resilient, a child whose brain is still developing is more likely than an adult to suffer long-lasting psychological damage from exposure to a traumatic event.

   b. People who suffer from post-traumatic stress disorder (PTSD) may experience intrusive recollections of the traumatic event, feel less emotionally responsive than before the event occurred, and feel increased anxiety, irritability, and anger.

6. a. Many men and women have become so obsessed with body image that they are willing to turn to drugs, fad diets, and even surgery to achieve their goals.

   b. Rising rates of eating disorders among young women and girls in the United States are almost certainly linked to the pervasiveness of images of very thin models and actresses in American popular culture.

7. a. Milestone Comics, which was launched in February 1993, issued more than 200 titles in the four years of its existence.

   b. The failure of Milestone Comics, which published comic books featuring black superheroes created and drawn by blacks, occurred because distributors believed that their white clientele would not buy comics about black characters who were not stereotypes.

8. a. Though many green energy companies have gone bankrupt in the past few years, the causes have primarily been poor management and fiscal irresponsibility rather than a fundamental problem with the industry.

   b. The federal government should not financially support green companies because these companies go bankrupt too often.

9. a. Empathy is one of the most important qualities a nurse can have; through empathy, a nurse can personally connect with and engage clients and also empower clients to work toward their own healing.

   b. This paper will answer the following question: What are some of the best methods for nurses to connect with their clients?

10. a. Gays, lesbians, and transgender people should not face discrimination in housing, employment, health benefits, financial benefits, or any other aspect of life.

    b. Because marriage entitles the partners to share insurance benefits and pay lower taxes, states that do not allow same-sex couples to marry are discriminating financially against gays, lesbians, and transgender people.

Hacker/Sommers, *Working with Sources: Exercises for Hacker Handbooks* (Boston: Bedford, 2018)

Thesis statements in APA papers 2

For help with this exercise, see the section on thesis statements in APA papers in your handbook.

Circle the letter of the sentence in each pair that would work well as the thesis statement for a research paper from five to ten pages long. Remember that a thesis should be a central idea that requires supporting evidence; it should be of adequate scope for a five- to ten-page paper; and it should be sharply focused.

EXAMPLE

(a.) Early-childhood intervention programs that focus on social and emotional development of disadvantaged youth deserve more funding because they have led to reductions in criminal behavior.

b. Early-childhood intervention programs for disadvantaged youth are very important.

1. a. More than one million school-aged children in the United States are educated primarily at home.

   b. Homeschooling is effective only when the correct social, emotional, and educational circumstances exist for both parent and child.

2. a. One way to ensure the early detection, effective treatment, and ultimate reduction of childhood mental health problems is to professionalize the child care industry.

   b. If we as a society don't do something to meet the mental health needs of very young children, we will all pay the price in the long run.

3. a. In 1997, the National Gambling Impact Study Commission found that the prevalence of pathological gambling was twice as likely to occur within 50 miles of a gambling facility.

   b. In Connecticut, where casino gambling and the state lottery contribute more than half a billion dollars a year to the state's revenue, more money should be spent on programs that can prevent and treat gambling addiction.

4. a. Although it has been criticized, the resource dilution model — the theory that the number of siblings a child has can influence his or her chances for intellectual development — offers the most likely explanation for why this causal relationship may exist.

   b. It is largely undisputed that children with no siblings are more likely to score higher on cognitive skills tests than children with multiple siblings.

5. a. The economic benefits of fracking are persuasive, but the social and environmental effects on Maryland's topography make the practice unjustifiable.

   b. Fracking in Virginia has been happening for 50 years, but in Maryland fracking would require more than 20 times the fracking liquid and would increase the risks of water pollution.

6. a. Most American parents, aware of the reality of teenage sexual activity, favor comprehensive sex education programs rather than abstinence-only programs for their children.

   b. Recent evidence suggests that abstinence-only sex education programs do not decrease the number of teenage pregnancies; in fact, these programs can actually increase the number of sexually transmitted diseases in teens because they do not incorporate discussions of safe sex.

7. a. Although many people believe that the number of suicides increases during times of severe economic crises, there is very little evidence to support this theory.

   b. Since the rate of suicides among Native American youths is more than twice the national average, federal agencies must make suicide prevention in our Native communities a top priority.

8. a. The pressure put on schools and educators for their students to perform well on standardized tests has resulted in higher scores but has not increased students' long-term ability to achieve.

   b. Proponents of the federal No Child Left Behind Act (NCLB) point to its emphasis on teacher accountability, its focus on quality education for all children, and its provision for school choice; but critics charge that NCLB is underfunded, narrowly focuses on three subject areas, and ultimately has lowered overall education standards.

9. a. Merit-based pay schemes base teacher salaries on performance, as most private-sector companies do, rather than on seniority, as most public school districts do.

   b. As can be seen in the success of many charter schools, using merit-based pay schemes for teachers is one way to bring about improved student performance.

10. a. Considering the enormous debt this country owes to its military personnel and their families, the government should support programs that help reduce domestic violence in military homes, where rates of child abuse and spousal abuse are above the national average.

    b. Domestic violence and substance abuse are much more prevalent in military families than in civilian families, especially during times of war.

Hacker/Sommers, *Working with Sources: Exercises for Hacker Handbooks* (Boston: Bedford, 2018)

Avoiding plagiarism in APA papers 1

For help with this exercise, see the section on avoiding plagiarism in APA papers in your handbook.

Read the following passage and the information about its source. Then decide whether each student sample is plagiarized or uses the source correctly. If the student's sample is plagiarized, write "plagiarized"; if the sample is acceptable, write "OK."

ORIGINAL SOURCE

For the sake of argument, let us consider the possibility that conscious mind is the "I" of each person, and can sometimes be in control. If one thinks of this as an avatar, the conscious mind avatar not only can control the subconscious but it can also control itself. Conscious mind can choose what to read, what people to associate with, what is good for the individual, what attitudes to hold and adjust, what to believe, and what to do. True, because of pre-existing subconscious programming, some conscious choices are more deterministic than others. But because of conscious mind, everyone can at least become aware of the price being paid for bad choices and have the option to change course, to change brain's programming accordingly.

It is clear that a brain avatar could make such choices. What is less clear is whether those choices are freely willed. . . . True, the avatar representations are often modified and biased by the output of subconscious programming, as evidence [*sic*] by mental "knee-jerk" responses.

From Klemm, W. R. (2011). Neural representations of the sense of self. *Advances in Cognitive Psychology, 7*(1), 16-30. doi:10.2478/v10053-008-0084-2 [The source passage is from page 22.]

1. The "I," or the conscious mind, of each person can be in control at times (Klemm, 2011, p. 22).

2. Klemm (2011) addressed the argument that free will is an illusion—that humans are programmed to make the choices they make—through his description of the "conscious mind avatar" (p. 22).

3. Because the conscious mind avatar is able to identify and choose what people to associate with, what to believe, and what to do, Klemm (2011) has suggested that humans have some control over their decisions (p. 22).

4. Though Klemm (2011) asserted that humans have some choice, he admitted that "because of . . . subconscious programming, some conscious choices are more deterministic than others" (p. 22).

5. We all understand that people are aware of the price they pay for bad choices and so can change course and alter the brain's programming (Klemm, 2011, p. 22).

6. As Klemm (2011) has suggested, the "brain avatar" could make decisions based on an understanding "of the price being paid for bad choices" (p. 22).

7. Though Klemm (2011) recognized that humans can make decisions based on their understanding of the consequences, he questioned whether those "choices" are freely willed (p. 22).

8. It is impossible to tell whether subconscious programming influences the decisions people think they make with free will.

9. Klemm (2011) asked whether a person making a decision based on relevant information is actually using free will or whether the subconscious is influencing the decision (p. 22).

10. While the "conscious mind avatar" can weigh evidence and decide the best course of action, decisions may be "modified and biased by . . . subconscious programming, as evidence [*sic*] by mental 'knee-jerk' responses" (Klemm, 2011, p. 22).

Avoiding plagiarism in APA papers 2

For help with this exercise, see the section on avoiding plagiarism in APA papers in your handbook.

Read the following passage and the information about its source. Then decide whether each student sample is plagiarized or uses the source correctly. If the student's sample is plagiarized, write "plagiarized"; if the sample is acceptable, write "OK."

ORIGINAL SOURCE

Incarceration has become a prominent American institution with substantial collateral consequences for families and communities, particularly among the most disadvantaged. . . . Simply stated, incarceration in America is concentrated among African American men. While 1 in every 87 white males ages 18 to 64 is incarcerated and the number for similarly-aged Hispanic males is 1 in 36, for black men it is 1 in 12. Moreover, . . . incarceration has implications for individual employment earnings and long-term economic mobility that are collectively amplified for minority communities, often already at a disadvantage in terms of broader financial well-being.

Other disparities surface when education is considered. In particular, those without a high school diploma or GED are far more likely to be locked up than others. While 1 in 57 white men ages 20 to 34 is incarcerated, the rate is 1 in 8 for white men of the same age group who lack a high school diploma or GED.

Black men, in particular, face enormously dim prospects when they fail to complete high school. More than one-third (37 percent) of black male dropouts between the ages of 20 and 34 are currently behind bars—three times the rate for whites in the same category. . . . This exceeds the share of young black male dropouts who have a job (26 percent). Thus, as adults in their twenties and early thirties, when they should be launching careers, black men without a high school diploma are more likely to be found in a cell than in the workplace.

The data about incarceration in America show that for many men growing up in the post-civil-rights era, prison looms as an increasingly predictable destination.

From Pew Charitable Trusts. (2010). *Collateral costs: Incarceration's effect on economic mobility.* Retrieved from http://www.pewtrusts.org/~/media/legacy/uploadedfiles/pcs _assets/2010/collateralcosts1pdf.pdf [The source passage is from pages 6 and 8; the second paragraph ends on page 6 and the third paragraph begins on page 8.]

1. According to a report by the Pew Charitable Trusts (2010), prison is an increasingly predictable destination for men—especially for black men (p. 8).

2. The results reported by the Pew Charitable Trusts (2010) are sobering: "While 1 in every 87 white males ages 18 to 64 is incarcerated and the number for similarly-aged Hispanic males is 1 in 36, for black men it is 1 in 12" (p. 6).

3. Research has shown that 1 in 57 young white males (20 to 34 years old) is in prison and that the rate for young white males of the same age *without* a high school diploma increases significantly—to 1 in 8 (p. 8).

4. Data reveal that when black men fail to complete high school, by the time they are 20 or 30 years old jail looks more and more likely (p. 8).

5. As a Pew Charitable Trusts (2010) report argued, incarceration has "substantial collateral consequences" for underprivileged individuals and communities, including disadvantages related to "financial well-being" and "long-term economic mobility" (p. 6).

Hacker/Sommers, *Working with Sources: Exercises for Hacker Handbooks* (Boston: Bedford, 2018)

Avoiding plagiarism in APA papers 3

For help with this exercise, see the section on avoiding plagiarism in APA papers in your handbook.

Read the following passage and the information about its source. Then decide whether each student sample is plagiarized or uses the source correctly. If the student sample is plagiarized, write "plagiarized"; if the sample is acceptable, write "OK."

ORIGINAL SOURCE

Mass psychogenic illness, or epidemic hysteria, is usually defined as a set of unexplained symptoms affecting two or more people; in most cases, victims share a theory of some sort about what is causing their distress. Often, somebody smells something funny, which may or may not be a chemical and which may or may not be there, but which in any case does not account for the subsequent symptoms. Relapses tend to happen when the people affected congregate again. And, notably, the mechanism of contagion is quite different from what you would expect in, say, a viral illness: symptoms spread by "line of sight," which is to say, people get sick as they see other people getting sick. Some element of unusual psychological stress is often at play. . . . Adolescents and preadolescents are particularly susceptible. And girls are more likely to fall ill than boys.

From Talbot, M. (2002, June 2). *Hysteria* hysteria. *The New York Times Magazine*, pp. 42-47, 58-59, 96, 98, 101-102. [The source passage is from pages 58-59. The word *Adolescents* begins page 59.]

1. Mass psychogenic illness, also known as epidemic hysteria, is a set of unexplained symptoms affecting two or more people who usually share a theory of some sort about what is causing their distress.

2. As Talbot (2002) has pointed out, victims of mass hysteria may believe that they have breathed in a strange odor that might or might not have been a toxic substance and that might or might not have been present; the chemical would not, in any case, explain the subsequent symptoms (p. 58).

3. In cases of mass hysteria, according to Talbot (2002), "Often, somebody smells something funny, which may or may not be a chemical and which may or may not be there, but which in any case does not account for the subsequent symptoms" (p. 58).

4. Talbot (2002) explained that people affected by an outbreak of epidemic hysteria usually "share a theory of some sort about what is causing their distress" (p. 58).

5. Talbot (2002) has described the peculiar nature of mass psychogenic illness, in which sufferers agree about the underlying cause—an odd smell, for example—of their physical symptoms and suffer relapses when they come in contact with other victims (p. 58).

6. People become ill when they see other people becoming ill, according to Talbot (2002), so the "mechanism of contagion" is not at all what you would expect in, for example, a viral ailment (p. 58).

7. According to Talbot (2002), epidemic hysteria differs in several ways from other contagious diseases; for example, relapses among victims tend to happen when the people affected congregate again (p. 58).

8. Talbot (2002) explained that mass psychogenic illness often afflicts people when they are under some kind of psychological pressure (p. 58).

9. Adolescents and preadolescents are particularly susceptible to mass hysteria, and girls are more likely to fall ill than boys are.

10. Talbot (2002) noted that certain groups of people most often succumb to epidemic hysteria—preadolescents and adolescents, especially, with girls more frequently affected than boys (p. 59).

Hacker/Sommers, *Working with Sources: Exercises for Hacker Handbooks* (Boston: Bedford, 2018)

Avoiding plagiarism in APA papers 4

For help with this exercise, see the section on avoiding plagiarism in APA papers in your handbook.

Read the following passage and the information about its source. Then decide whether each student sample is plagiarized or uses the source correctly. If the student sample is plagiarized, write "plagiarized"; if the sample is acceptable, write "OK."

ORIGINAL SOURCE

While Easter Island was divided into about eleven territories, each belonging to one clan under its own chief and competing with other clans, the island was also loosely integrated religiously, economically, and politically under the leadership of one paramount chief. On other Polynesian islands, competition between chiefs for prestige could take the form of inter-island efforts such as trading and raiding, but Easter's extreme isolation from other islands precluded that possibility. Instead, the excellent quality of Rano Raraku volcanic stone for carving eventually resulted in chiefs competing by erecting statues representing their high-ranking ancestors on rectangular stone platforms (termed *ahu*).

From Diamond, J. (2004, March 25). Twilight at Easter [Review of the books *The enigmas of Easter Island*, by J. Flenly & P. Bahn, and *Among stone giants: The life of Katherine Routledge and her remarkable expedition to Easter Island*, by J. A. Van Tilburg]. *The New York Review of Books, 51*(5), 6, 8-10. [The source paragraph appears on page 8.]

1. Diamond (2004) explained that the 11 territories on Easter Island were "loosely integrated religiously, economically, and politically" under the leadership of one paramount chief (p. 8).

2. Easter Island was more isolated than other Polynesian islands, and therefore its chiefs did not compete with chiefs from other islands, as was typical elsewhere in the South Pacific (Diamond, 2004, p. 8).

3. Diamond (2004) observed that "Easter Island was divided into about eleven territories, each belonging to one clan under its own chief and competing with other clans" (p. 8).

4. According to Diamond (2004), rivalries between Polynesian rulers for status sometimes took the form of island-to-island endeavors like commerce or invasions.

5. Diamond (2004) noted that rather than compete with chiefs on other Polynesian islands, Easter Island's chiefs competed among themselves by erecting statues representing their high-ranking ancestors.

Recognizing common knowledge in APA papers

For help with this exercise, see the section on recognizing common knowledge in APA papers in your handbook.

Read the student passage and determine whether the student needs to cite the source of the information in an APA paper. If the material does not need citation because it is common knowledge, write "common knowledge." If the material is not common knowledge and the student should cite the source, write "needs citation."

EXAMPLE

Sigmund Freud believed that dreams provide clues about the dreamer's psychological conflicts. *Common Knowledge* [This general fact about Freud's ideas is widely known in the social sciences.]

1. In double-blind trials to test the effectiveness of St. John's wort as an antidepressant, the plant performed no better than a placebo.

2. In 2012, Ben Bernanke was the chair of the Federal Reserve Board.

3. In both 2011 and 2012, the most popular name given to baby girls in the United States was Sophia.

4. Phrenology, the study of bumps on the skull, advanced scientists' understanding of the ways different parts of the brain function.

5. The sense of smell and the sense of taste are linked.

6. When the Homestead Act took effect, granting 160 acres of western land to any head of a household—male or female—who would live there and improve it for five years, women filed 10% of the claims.

7. Babe Ruth's record for home runs in a single season was not broken for decades.

8. Many California earthquakes occur along the San Andreas Fault.

9. Studies have shown that unlike elderly Americans, who tend to become more forgetful as they age, elderly people in mainland China have memories as good as those of younger people in their culture.

10. Anorexia and bulimia are disorders affecting more young women than young men.

Hacker/Sommers, *Working with Sources: Exercises for Hacker Handbooks* (Boston: Bedford, 2018)

Integrating sources in APA papers 1

For help with this exercise, see the section on integrating sources in APA papers in your handbook.

Read the following passage and the information about its source. Then decide whether each student sample uses the source correctly. If the student has made an error in using the source, revise the sample to avoid the error. If the student has quoted correctly, write "OK."

ORIGINAL SOURCE

Even the most conscientious agriculture has some environmental impact, and though much food production yields greenhouse gases, raising livestock has a much higher potential for global warming than crop farming. For example: To produce one calorie of corn takes 2.2 calories of fossil fuel. For beef the number is 40: *it requires 40 calories to produce one calorie of beef protein.*

In other words, if you grow corn and eat it, you expend 2.2 calories of energy in order to eat one of protein. But if you process that corn, and feed it to a steer, and take into account all the other needs that steer has through its lifetime—land use, chemical fertilizers (largely petroleum-based), pesticides, machinery, transport, drugs, water, and so on—you're responsible for 40 calories of energy to get that same calorie of protein. According to one estimate, a typical steer consumes the equivalent of 135 gallons of gasoline in his lifetime, enough for even some gas guzzlers to drive more than halfway from New York to Los Angeles, or for an energy-efficient car to make the drive back and forth twice. Or try to imagine each cow on the planet consuming almost seven barrels of crude oil.

From Bittman, M. (2009). *Food matters: A guide to conscious eating with more than 75 recipes.* New York, NY: Simon & Schuster. [The source passage is on pages 16-17. Page 16 ends with *petroleum-*, and page 17 starts with *based.*]

1. Bittman (2009) made a strong environmental argument for preferring raising crops to raising and processing meat (pp. 16-17).

2. It takes 2.2 calories of fossil fuel to produce one calorie of edible corn, while it takes 40 calories to produce one calorie of beef protein (Bittman, 2009, p. 16).

3. Bittman (2009) argued that one reason to avoid eating meat is that producing meat uses up many more resources than does eating a plant-based diet (pp. 16-17).

4. The resources needed to grow livestock are astonishing. According to Bittman (2009), "To produce one calorie of corn takes 2.2 calories of fossil fuel. For beef the number is 40" (p. 16).

5. Bittman (2009) explained that "if you process that corn, and feed it to a steer, and take into account all the other needs that steer has through its lifetime—you're responsible for 40 calories of energy to get the same calorie of protein" (pp. 16-17).

6. Bittman (2009) came down firmly on the side of plant-based agriculture (as opposed to raising livestock), comparing the energy used to raise a single steer to the fuel needed to drive halfway across the country (p. 17).

7. Bittman (2009) argued against raising livestock: Imagine every cow in the world using seven barrels of crude oil (p. 17).

8. Raising livestock takes more energy than does raising vegetables. "If you process . . . corn, and feed it to a steer, and take into account all the other needs that steer has through its lifetime — land use, chemical fertilizers (largely petroleum-based), pesticides, machinery, transport, drugs, water, and so on — you're responsible for 40 calories of energy to get the same calorie of protein" (Bittman, 2009, pp. 16-17).

9. According to Bittman (2009), beef-eaters are "responsible for 40 calories of energy to get [one] calorie of protein" (p. 17).

10. In terms of fossil-fuel usage, Bittman (2009) compared the energy required to raise a steer for food consumption to the gasoline used in "driving from New York to Los Angeles in an energy-efficient car . . . twice" (p. 17).

Hacker/Sommers, *Working with Sources: Exercises for Hacker Handbooks* (Boston: Bedford, 2018)

Integrating sources in APA papers 2

For help with this exercise, see the section on integrating sources in APA papers in your handbook.

Read the following passage and the information about its source. Then decide whether each student sample uses the source correctly. If the student has made an error in using the source, revise the sample to avoid the error. If the student has quoted correctly, write "OK."

ORIGINAL SOURCE

Perhaps the book that has most helped us understand why low-income women would choose to have children but not marry is Kathryn Edin and Maria Kefalas' *Promises I Can Keep: Why Poor Women Put Motherhood Before Marriage* (2005). According to Edin and Kefalas, the movement away from marriage, which has been profound among low-income women, is not about abandoning marriage as an ideal. They agree with [sociologist Andrew] Cherlin that marriage has great symbolic value among the poor women they interview. These women hope to marry and they want a stable two-parent family and all its trappings as much as their more advantaged peers. But it is out of reach for them.

What these women are not willing to forego [*sic*] is having children. If they were to wait until they had good prospects for a stable marriage, it might mean remaining childless. Children bring meaning, give purpose to life. Once they have children, they want other things in place before considering marriage. They want to have some economic independence so that they have a say in their relationships with men. They also want to make sure that the men in their lives can be trusted on a number of dimensions—trusted to put the interests of family first by getting and keeping a job, staying off drugs, staying out of jail, remaining faithful, and not physically abusing them.

From Bianchi, S. M. (2013, May 20). The more they change, the more they stay the same? Understanding family change in the twenty-first century. *Contemporary Sociology, 42*(3), 324-331. doi:10.1177/0094306113484700 [The source passage is from page 326.]

1. Bianchi (2013) cited research from Edin and Kefalas, which argued that marriage "has great symbolic value among the poor" (p. 326).

2. Bianchi (2013) noted that though the women interviewed by Edin and Kefalas have remained single, they still want to get married (p. 326).

3. Women living in poverty "hope to marry and they want a stable two-parent family and all its trappings as much as their more advantaged peers" (Bianchi, 2013, p. 326).

4. Bianchi (2013) explained that while poor women believe in marriage for themselves, "they want to have some economic independence" before marriage "so that they have a say in their relationships with men" (p. 326).

5. Bianchi (2013) noted that the women interviewed need to know that men "can be trusted to put the interests of family first" and can lead stable lives (p. 326).

Integrating sources in APA papers 3

For help with this exercise, see the section on integrating sources in APA papers in your handbook.

Read the following passage and the information about its source. Then decide whether each student sample uses the source correctly. If the student has made an error in using the source, revise the sample to avoid the error. If the student has quoted correctly, write "OK."

ORIGINAL SOURCE

According to their scores on achievement tests, which correlate closely with IQ, GED★ recipients were every bit as smart as high-school graduates. But when Heckman★★ looked at their path through higher education, he discovered that GED recipients weren't *anything* like high-school graduates. At age twenty-two, Heckman found, just 3 percent of GED recipients were enrolled in a four-year university or had completed some kind of post-secondary degree, compared to 46 percent of high-school graduates. In fact, Heckman discovered that when you consider all kinds of important future outcomes—annual income, unemployment rate, divorce rate, use of illegal drugs—GED recipients look exactly like high-school dropouts, despite the fact that they have earned this supposedly valuable extra credential, and despite the fact that they are, on average, considerably more intelligent than high-school dropouts.

Tough, P. (2012). *How children succeed: Grit, curiosity, and the hidden power of character.* Boston, MA: Houghton Mifflin. [The source paragraph is from page xviii.]

★GED (General Educational Development), a test of academic competence at a high school level.

★★James Heckman, an economist and a Nobel Prize recipient, whose research focuses in part on educational development.

1. It is a misperception that GED recipients are unintelligent; as Tough (2012) noted, "according to their scores on achievement tests, GED recipients were every bit as smart as high-school graduates" (p. xviii).

2. Most GED recipients did not continue their education after receiving their certificates. "At age twenty-two, . . . just 3 percent of GED recipients were enrolled in a four-year university" (Tough, 2012, p. xviii).

3. For some measures of success, Tough (2012) explained that "GED recipients look exactly like high-school dropouts" (p. xviii).

4. Tough (2012) cited research showing that while almost half of high school graduates went on to higher education at some level, only 3% of GED recipients did so (p. xviii).

5. Tough (2012) noted that GED recipients are, on average, considerably more intelligent than high-school dropouts, although their "important future outcomes" are no different from those of dropouts (p. xviii).

Hacker/Sommers, *Working with Sources: Exercises for Hacker Handbooks* (Boston: Bedford, 2018)

Integrating sources in APA papers 4

For help with this exercise, see the section on integrating sources in APA papers in your handbook.

Read the following passage and the information about its source. Then decide whether each student sample uses the source correctly. If the student has made an error in using the source, revise the sample to avoid the error. If the student has quoted correctly, write "OK."

ORIGINAL SOURCE

Mental-health workers have long theorized that it takes grueling emotional exertion to recover from the death of a loved one. So-called grief work, now the stock-in-trade of a growing number of grief counselors, entails confronting the reality of a loved one's demise and grappling with the harsh emotions triggered by that loss.

Two new studies, however, knock grief work off its theoretical pedestal. Among bereaved spouses tracked for up to 2 years after their partners' death, those who often talked with others and briefly wrote in diaries about their emotions fared no better than their tight-lipped, unexpressive counterparts, according to psychologist Margaret Stroebe of Utrecht University in the Netherlands and her colleagues.

From Bower, B. (2002, March 2). Good grief: Bereaved adjust well without airing emotion. *Science News, 161,* 131-132. [The source passage is from page 131.]

1. Researchers at Utrecht University found that bereaved spouses who often talked with others and briefly wrote in diaries about their emotions fared no better than their tight-lipped, unexpressive counterparts (Bower, 2002, p. 131).

2. Researchers at Utrecht University found that bereaved spouses "who often talked with others and briefly wrote in diaries fared no better than their tight-lipped, unexpressive counterparts" (Bower, 2002, p. 131).

3. Psychologist Margaret Stroebe and her colleagues found that bereaved spouses "who often talked with others and briefly wrote in diaries . . . fared no better than their tight-lipped, unexpressive counterparts" (Bower, 2002, p. 131).

4. According to Bower (2002), "Mental-health workers have always believed that it takes grueling emotional exertion to recover from a loved one's death" (p. 131).

5. Mental-health professionals have assumed that people stricken by grief need a great deal of help. "So-called grief work, now the stock-in-trade of a growing number of grief counselors, entails confronting the reality of a loved one's demise and grappling with the harsh emotions triggered by that loss" (Bower, 2002, p. 131).

6. Bower (2002) has observed that recent studies of bereaved spouses "knock grief work off its theoretical pedestal" (p. 131).

7. Bower (2002) has described grief counselors as helping the bereaved "[confront] the reality of a loved one's demise and [grapple] with the harsh emotions triggered by that loss" (p. 131).

8. Researchers at Utrecht University find no difference in the speed of adapting to a spouse's death among subjects "who often talked with others and briefly wrote in diaries" and "their tight-lipped, unexpressive counterparts" (Bower, 2002, p. 131).

9. Bower (2002) noted that new studies may change the common perception of how people recover from grief:

   "Among bereaved spouses tracked for up to 2 years after their partners' death, those who often talked with others and briefly wrote in diaries about their emotions fared no better than their tight-lipped, unexpressive counterparts, according to psychologist Margaret Stroebe of Utrecht University in the Netherlands and her colleagues." (p. 131)

10. "Mental-health workers have long theorized that it takes grueling emotional exertion to recover from the death of a loved one," reported Bower (2002), but "new studies . . . knock grief work off its theoretical pedestal" (p. 131).

Hacker/Sommers, *Working with Sources: Exercises for Hacker Handbooks* (Boston: Bedford, 2018)

APA documentation: in-text citations 1

For help with this exercise, see the APA in-text citations section in your handbook.

Circle the letter of the APA in-text citation that is handled correctly.

EXAMPLE

The student is quoting from the following article:

More bad brain news in football. (2012). *ASHA Leader, 17*(13), 3.

(a.) Research has shown that NFL "players were three times more likely than the general population to die from diseases that damage brain cells" ("More Bad Brain News," 2012, p. 3).

b. Research has shown that NFL "players were three times more likely than the general population to die from diseases that damage brain cells" (*ASHA Leader*, 2012, p. 3).

1. The student is quoting from page 44 of the following article:

   McGrath, B. (2011, January 31). Does football have a future? The N.F.L. and the concussion crisis. *The New Yorker, 86*(46), 40-51.

   a. In discussing the prevalence of long-term brain injury in professional athletes, McGrath (2011) noted that "Dr. Maroon has delineated four stages in the N.F.L.'s reaction to the reality of brain damage: active resistance and passive resistance, shifting to passive acceptance and, finally, in the past few months, active acceptance" (p. 44).

   b. In discussing the prevalence of long-term brain injury in professional athletes, McGrath noted that "Dr. Maroon has delineated four stages in the N.F.L.'s reaction to the reality of brain damage: active resistance and passive resistance, shifting to passive acceptance and, finally, in the past few months, active acceptance" (2011, p. 44).

2. The student is quoting from page 1295 of the following article. It is the first time the source has been cited in the paper.

   DeKosky, S. T., Ikonomovic, M. D., & Gandy, S. (2010). Traumatic brain injury—Football, warfare, and long-term effects. *The New England Journal of Medicine, 363*, 1293-1296.

   a. The authors explained that in sports like football and wrestling, head injuries are ignored so players can continue to play, while in boxing, "knockouts are recorded as part of scoring" (DeKosky, Ikonomovic, & Gandy, 2010, p. 1295).

   b. The authors explained that in sports like football and wrestling, head injuries are ignored so players can continue to play, while in boxing, "knockouts are recorded as part of scoring" (DeKosky et al., 2010, p. 1295).

3. The student is quoting from page 8 in the following book:

Nowinski, C. (2006). *Head games: Football's concussion crisis from the NFL to youth leagues.* East Bridgewater, MA: Drummond Group.

a. In his research, Nowinski (2006) found that "former NFL players had a 37 percent greater chance of developing Alzheimer's disease than an average person" (8).

b. In his research, Nowinski (2006) found that "former NFL players had a 37 percent greater chance of developing Alzheimer's disease than an average person" (p. 8).

4. The student is paraphrasing information from the following book:

Carroll, L., & Rosner, D. (2011). *The concussion crisis: Anatomy of a silent epidemic.* New York, NY: Simon & Schuster.

a. Carroll and Rosner (2011, p. 115) give two reasons for the rise in concussions among recent veterans: More explosive devices are being used by insurgents in Iraq and Afghanistan than in previous conflicts, and wounds that would have killed a soldier in the past are being successfully treated because of better medical practices.

b. Carroll and Rosner (2011) give two reasons for the rise in concussions among recent veterans: More explosive devices are being used by insurgents in Iraq and Afghanistan than in previous conflicts, and wounds that would have killed a soldier in the past are being successfully treated because of better medical practices (p. 115).

5. The student is paraphrasing information from the following radio interview:

Nowinski, C. (2011, January 20). Brain injuries haunt football players years later [Interview by D. Davies]. Retrieved from http://npr.org/

a. Nowinski explained that the data did not make people take notice. The stories of former NFL athletes who suffered from postconcussion syndrome made the public realize there was a crisis (Nowinski & Davies, 2011).

b. Nowinski (2011) explained that the data did not make people take notice. The stories of former NFL athletes who suffered from postconcussion syndrome made the public realize there was a crisis.

Hacker/Sommers, *Working with Sources: Exercises for Hacker Handbooks* (Boston: Bedford, 2018)

6. The student is paraphrasing and quoting from page 116 of the following testimony at a congressional hearing:

> Goodell, R. S. (2009, October 28). *Legal issues relating to football head injuries (Part I & II)*. Testimony before the Committee on the Judiciary, House of Representatives. Retrieved from http://judiciary.house.gov/hearings/hear_091028.html

a. When Representative Linda Sánchez expressed her belief that the NFL ignored crucial evidence about concussions in football, Roger Goodell (2009), commissioner of the National Football League, countered that the NFL "to a large extent [has] driven this issue" (p. 116).

b. When Representative Linda Sánchez expressed her belief that the NFL ignored crucial evidence about concussions in football, Roger Goodell (2009), commissioner of the National Football League, countered that the NFL "to a large extent [has] driven this issue."

7. The student is quoting from the following online article (the article is unpaginated):

> Malloy, D. (2009, October 29). Hearing spotlights NFL concussions. *Pittsburgh Post-Gazette*. Retrieved from http://www.post-gazette.com/

a. Malloy (2009) noted that a full day of testimony resulted in "no clear solution . . . amid discussions of brain scans, collective bargaining and lives cut short."

b. Malloy noted that a full day of testimony resulted in "no clear solution . . . amid discussions of brain scans, collective bargaining and lives cut short" (2009, n.p.).

8. The student is quoting from page 245 of the following journal article. It is the first time the source has been cited in the paper.

> Baugh, C. M., Stamm, J. M., Riley, D. O., Gavett, B. E., Shenton, M. E., Lin, A., . . . Stern, R. A. (2012). Chronic traumatic encephalopathy: Neurodegeneration following repetitive concussive and subconcussive brain trauma. *Brain Imaging and Behavior, 6*(2), 244-254.

a. There is a clear difference between post-concussive syndrome and chronic traumatic encephalopathy (CTE), as Baugh et al. (2012) explained: "Post-concussive syndrome symptoms endure following an acute concussion without complete relief of symptoms of the initial injury, [while] the symptoms of CTE typically do not present until years after the trauma-producing activity, and the symptoms of initial injury, if any, have ended" (p. 245).

b. There is a clear difference between post-concussive syndrome and chronic traumatic encephalopathy (CTE), as Baugh, Stamm, Riley, Gavett, Shenton, Lin, and Stern (2012) explained: "Post-concussive syndrome symptoms endure following an acute concussion without complete relief of symptoms of the initial injury, [while] the symptoms of CTE typically do not present until years after the trauma-producing activity, and the symptoms of initial injury, if any, have ended" (p. 245).

9. The student is paraphrasing information from the following radio interview:

> Cantu, R. (2012, September 8). Hit counts seen as path to safer sports [Interview by
> B. Littlefield]. Retrieved from http://onlyagame.wbur.org/

a. Cantu explained that both neuropsychological and physical evidence has shown that hits to the head that do not result in concussion symptoms still negatively affect the brain (2012).

b. Cantu (2012) explained that both neuropsychological and physical evidence has shown that hits to the head that do not result in concussion symptoms still negatively affect the brain.

10. The student is paraphrasing information from the following unpaginated online article:

> Ritter, M. (2012, September 9). Study: Brain disease deaths high in NFL veterans.
> *Boston Globe*. Retrieved from http://boston.com/

a. Ritter (2012) noted that one problem with the study was that researchers did not test for chronic traumatic encephalopathy because it is not a major cause of death.

b. Ritter noted that one problem with the study was that researchers did not test for chronic traumatic encephalopathy because it is not a major cause of death.

Hacker/Sommers, *Working with Sources: Exercises for Hacker Handbooks* (Boston: Bedford, 2018)

APA documentation: in-text citations 2

For help with this exercise, see the APA in-text citations section in your handbook.

Circle the letter of the APA in-text citation that is handled correctly.

EXAMPLE

The student is quoting from a blog by pediatrician Nadine Burke Harris. The blog entry is undated.

a. Pediatrician Nadine Burke Harris stated that her clinical experience shows that child-parent psychotherapy "is best practice doing healing work with children experiencing toxic stress."

b. Pediatrician Nadine Burke Harris (n.d.) stated that her clinical experience shows that child-parent psychotherapy "is best practice doing healing work with children experiencing toxic stress."

1. The student is citing a quotation by Elizabeth Dozier on page 5 of a book by Paul Tough. The book was published in 2012.

   a. Dozier explained her change of heart: "The reality is that . . . you can't expect to solve the problems of a school without taking into account what's happening in the community" (as cited in Tough, 2012, p. 5).

   b. Dozier explained her change of heart: "The reality is that . . . you can't expect to solve the problems of a school without taking into account what's happening in the community" (Tough, 2012, p. 5).

2. The student is paraphrasing information from an article by Jamie L. Hanson, Moo K. Chung, Brian B. Avants, Karen D. Rudolph, Elizabeth A. Shirtcliff, James C. Gee, Richard J. Davidson, and Seth D. Pollak that was published on the unpaginated website of an academic journal in 2012.

   a. The study conducted by Hanson, Chung, Avants, Rudolph, Shirtcliff, Gee, Davidson, and Pollak suggests that cumulative life stress, especially that experienced in adolescence, impairs cognitive performance (2012).

   b. The study conducted by Hanson et al. (2012) suggests that cumulative life stress, especially that experienced in adolescence, impairs cognitive performance.

3. The student is quoting from an article by Jack P. Shonkoff that appeared on page 982 of a 2011 issue of *Science*.

   a. Shonkoff argued that "when young children are burdened by significant adversity, stress response systems are overactivated, maturing brain circuits can be impaired, and metabolic regulatory systems and developing organs can be disrupted, and the probabilities increase for long-term problems in learning" (2011, p. 982).

b. Shonkoff (2011) argued that "when young children are burdened by significant adversity, stress response systems are overactivated, maturing brain circuits can be impaired, and metabolic regulatory systems and developing organs can be disrupted, and the probabilities increase for long-term problems in learning" (p. 982).

4. The student is quoting from Figure 1 on page S68 of an article written by Andrew S. Garner in 2013.

   a. Garner (2013) presented childhood adversity on a continuum from positive to tolerable to toxic stress, the latter of which "links adversity with poor health and health disparities" (Figure 1, p. S68).

   b. Garner (2013) presented childhood adversity on a continuum from positive to tolerable to toxic stress, the latter of which "links adversity with poor health and health disparities" (Figure 1).

5. The student is quoting information from page 1 of a clinical report published in 2008 and written by Horacio Hojman.

   a. Hojman (2008) warned that doctors should not misdiagnose PTSD as ADHD, noting that "for concentration problems and distractability to be attributed to ADHD, they should have existed before the age of 7, been evident before the trauma occurred, be relatively chronic and generally be worse in the school setting" (p. 1).

   b. H. Hojman (2008) warned that doctors should not misdiagnose PTSD as ADHD, noting that "for concentration problems and distractability to be attributed to ADHD, they should have existed before the age of 7, been evident before the trauma occurred, be relatively chronic and generally be worse in the school setting" (p. 1).

6. The student is quoting Jamie Hanson, whose words were included in an article written by Chris Barncard and published on an unpaginated website in 2012.

   a. Hanson explained the results of the study: "We have now found . . . that more exposure to stress is related to more issues with certain kinds of cognitive processes" (as cited in Barncard, 2012).

   b. Hanson explained the results of the study: "We have now found . . . that more exposure to stress is related to more issues with certain kinds of cognitive processes" (as cited in Barncard).

7. The student is quoting from an article written by Arielle Levin Becker and published on an unpaginated website in 2017.

   a. Since traumatic experiences such as abuse "affect brain development, learning, relationships, and health, young children are particularly vulnerable to the effects" (Becker, 2017).

   b. Since traumatic experiences such as abuse "affect brain development, learning, relationships, and health, young children are particularly vulnerable to the effects" (Becker, 2017, n.p.).

Hacker/Sommers, *Working with Sources: Exercises for Hacker Handbooks* (Boston: Bedford, 2018)

8. The student is paraphrasing a video interview with pediatrician Nadine Burke Harris that was posted on the Zócalo Public Square YouTube page in 2012.

   a. Harris (2012), a pediatrician who works with a large population of at-risk youth, explained that children who experience traumatic events are more likely to suffer from diseases such as hepatitis and are more likely to attempt suicide.

   b. Harris, a pediatrician who works with a large population of at-risk youth, explained that children who experience traumatic events are more likely to suffer from diseases such as hepatitis and are more likely to attempt suicide (Zócalo Public Square, 2012).

9. The student is quoting from page 259 of a book by Marjorie J. Kostelnik, Kara Murphy Gregory, Anne K. Soderman, and Alice Phipps Whiren that was published in 2012. This is the second reference to this source in the paper.

   a. Kostelnik, Gregory, Soderman, and Whiren (2012) noted that as many as "25% of all children are at risk of academic failure because of physical, emotional, or social problems and are less able to function well in the classroom because they are hungry, sick, troubled, or depressed" (p. 259).

   b. Kostelnik et al. (2012) noted that as many as "25% of all children are at risk of academic failure because of physical, emotional, or social problems and are less able to function well in the classroom because they are hungry, sick, troubled, or depressed" (p. 259).

10. The student is quoting from a news release posted by the Eunice Kennedy Shriver National Institute of Child Health and Human Development (NICHD). The release was published online on August 28, 2012. This is the second mention of the source in the paper.

    a. Research has shown that "high levels of stress hormones influence the developing circuitry of children's brains, inhibiting . . . higher cognitive functions such as planning, impulse and emotional control, and attention" (Eunice Kennedy Shriver National Institute of Child Health and Human Development, 2012).

    b. Research has shown that "high levels of stress hormones influence the developing circuitry of children's brains, inhibiting . . . higher cognitive functions such as planning, impulse and emotional control, and attention" (NICHD, 2012).

APA documentation: in-text citations 3

For help with this exercise, see the APA in-text citations section in your handbook.

Circle the letter of the APA in-text citation that is handled correctly.

EXAMPLE

The student is quoting from page 15 of a working paper written by Andrew Cook, Martin Gaynor, Melvin Stephens Jr., and Lowell Taylor and published in 2012. This is the first reference to the source in the paper.

a. While the authors admitted that it was difficult to generalize "causal inferences" based on the results of their studies, they explained that "those hospitals that are most effective in ensuring patient safety generally find it optimal to employ more nurses per patient" (Cook, Gaynor, Stephens, & Taylor, 2012, p. 15).

b. While the authors (2012) admitted that it was difficult to generalize "causal inferences" based on the results of their studies, they explained that "those hospitals that are most effective in ensuring patient safety generally find it optimal to employ more nurses per patient" (Cook, Gaynor, Stephens, & Taylor, p. 15).

1. The student is quoting Senator Barbara Boxer, who was quoted in a blog written by Pete Kasperowicz and published in 2013.

    a. When Boxer introduced legislation to mandate a lower nurse-to-patient ratio, she said, "We must support the nurses who work tirelessly every day to provide the best possible care to their patients" (quoted in Kasperowicz, 2013).

    b. When Boxer introduced legislation to mandate a lower nurse-to-patient ratio, she said, "We must support the nurses who work tirelessly every day to provide the best possible care to their patients" (as cited in Kasperowicz, 2013).

2. The student is paraphrasing information from an article by Joanne Spetz, Nancy Donaldson, Carolyn Aydin, and Diane S. Brown that was published on an unpaginated website in 2008. This is the first citation of the source in the paper.

    a. Spetz, Donaldson, Aydin, & Brown (2008) explained that one of the problems in collecting data on nurse-to-patient ratios is that payroll hours might not reflect nurses working in multiple departments during a single shift.

    b. Spetz, Donaldson, Aydin, and Brown (2008) explained that one of the problems in collecting data on nurse-to-patient ratios is that payroll hours might not reflect nurses working in multiple departments during a single shift.

3. The student is quoting from page 1861 of an academic journal article written by Ravi K. Amaravadi, Justin B. Dimick, Peter J. Pronovost, and Pamela A. Lipsett that was published in 2000. This is the second citation of the source in the paper.

   a. Amaravadi et al. (2000) concluded that for postoperative patients, "reducing costs by reducing nurse staffing [in the ICU] may . . . be counter-productive" (p. 1861).

   b. Amaravadi, Dimick, Pronovost, and Lipsett (2000) concluded that for postoperative patients, "reducing costs by reducing nurse staffing [in the ICU] may . . . be counter-productive" (p. 1861).

4. The student is paraphrasing and quoting information from pages 88-90 of a book written by Suzanne Gordon, John Buchanan, and Tanya Bretherton that was published in 2008. The paraphrase encompasses pages 88-90; the direct quotation is from page 88. This is the first time the student has cited this source.

   a. While hospitals insist that technological advances reduce the need for low nursing ratios, nurses have found that inaccuracy and glitches often make the technology more "onerous, rather than time-saving" (Gordon, Buchanan, & Bretherton, 2008, p. 88).

   b. While hospitals insist that technological advances reduce the need for such low nursing ratios, nurses have found that inaccuracy and glitches often make the technology more "onerous, rather than time-saving" (Gordon, Buchanan, & Bretherton, 2008, pp. 88-90).

5. The student quotes from a letter to the editor published in 2010 on a newspaper's unpaginated website. The letter was written by Marilyn Jaffe-Ruiz.

   a. Marilyn Jaffe-Ruiz (2010) responded to the *Times* story by saying that "legislation would help prevent 'failure to rescue,' a term used for tragic patient outcomes because a nurse is too busy to respond. It would also increase job satisfaction, a crucial element to retaining nurses."

   b. Marilyn Jaffe-Ruiz (2010) responded to the *Times* story by saying that "legislation would help prevent 'failure to rescue,' a term used for tragic patient outcomes because a nurse is too busy to respond. It would also increase job satisfaction, a crucial element to retaining nurses" (n.p.).

Hacker/Sommers, *Working with Sources: Exercises for Hacker Handbooks* (Boston: Bedford, 2018)

APA documentation: identifying elements of sources

For help with this exercise, see the APA identifying elements of sources section in your handbook.

Circle the correct answer for each question, using information in the source provided.

SOURCE: AN EDITION OTHER THAN THE FIRST

[Title page]

Cognitive Psychology and Its Implications
Sixth Edition

John R. Anderson
Carnegie Mellon University

Worth Publishers

[Copyright page]

TO GORDON BOWER

Sponsoring Editor: Laura Pople
Development Editor: Melissa Mashburn
Assistant Editor: Danielle Storm
Marketing Manager: Katherine Nurre
Project Editor: Georgia Lee Hadler
Manuscript Editors: Diana Siemens and Patricia Zimmerman
Production Manager: Sarah Segal
Art Director: Barbara Reingold
Cover/Text Designer: Lissi Sigillo
New Media and Supplements Editor: Danielle Pucci
Photo Editor: Ted Szczepanski
Composition: Macmillan India Ltd.
Printing and Binding: R. R. Donnelley and Sons
Cover Illustration: At the Sign of the Red Fish...
Soldati, The Art Arc...
Chapter Opening I...
LifeART image ©19...
reserved. MRI in pr...
back image from Te...

Library of Congre...
Anderson, John R. ...
  Cognitive psychol...
  p. cm.
  Includes bibliogra...
  ISBN: 0-7167-0110...
  1. Cognition—Te...

BF11.A5895 2004
153—dc22

> ©2005, 2000, 1995, 1990, 1985, 1980 by Worth
> W. H. Freeman and Company
>
> All rights reserved.
> Printed in the United States of America.
>
> First printing 2004
>
> Worth Publishers
> 41 Madison Avenue
> New York, NY 10010
> www.worthpublishers.com

2004054990

ISBN: 0-7167-0110-3   EAN: 9780716701101

©2005, 2000, 1995, 1990, 1985, 1980 by Worth Publishers and
W. H. Freeman and Company

All rights reserved.
Printed in the United States of America.

First printing 2004

Worth Publishers
41 Madison Avenue
New York, NY 10010
www.worthpublishers.com

Faculty Services: (800) 446-8923

Technical Support: (800) 936-6899

1. How would you begin an APA reference list entry for this source?

   a. Anderson, J. R. (2005).

   b. Anderson, J. R. (1980).

2. How would you cite the title and publisher for this source in an APA reference list entry?

   a. *Cognitive Psychology and Its Implications*. New York, NY: Worth.

   b. *Cognitive psychology and its implications* (6th ed.). New York, NY: Worth.

[Title page]

body outlaws
body outlaws

rewriting the rules
of beauty and body image

edited by ophira edut
foreword by rebecca walker

seal press

[First page of chapter]

of the art ponytail
the art of the ponytail
akkida mcdowell

My crowning glory is a war zone. Every day I wake up prepared
do battle, to fight both for and against the enemy that lies on top
my head.

For years, I clashed with my hair. I struggled to make it mi

3. You have used the chapter on the right from the collection whose title page is on the left. What information would come first in your APA reference list entry?

   a. McDowell, A.

   b. Edut, O. (Ed.).

4. What is the correct APA reference list entry for this source? The book was published in Emeryville, California, in 2003; the chapter begins on page 124 and ends on page 132.

   a. Edut, O. (Ed.). (2003). *Body Outlaws: Rewriting the Rules of Beauty and Body Image* (pp. 124-132). Emeryville, CA: Seal Press.

   b. McDowell, A. (2003). The art of the ponytail. In O. Edut (Ed.), *Body outlaws: Rewriting the rules of beauty and body image* (pp. 124-132). Emeryville, CA: Seal Press.

SOURCE: AN ARTICLE FROM A DATABASE

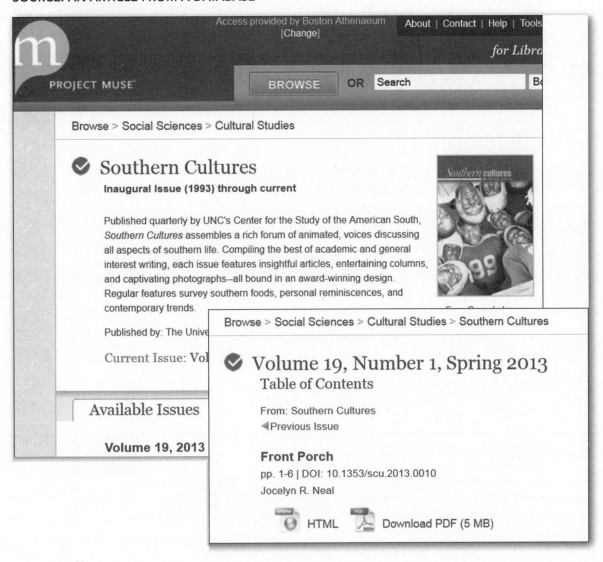

5. How would you begin an APA reference list entry for this article from a database?

   a. Neal, J. R. (2013). Front porch.

   b. Neal, J. R. (2013). "Front porch."

6. How would you cite the publication information for the periodical in this database record? (Each issue of the volume begins on page 1.)

   a. *Southern Cultures, 19*(1), 1-6.

   b. *Southern Cultures, 19* (2013): 1-6.

7. How would you end the reference list entry for this source?

   a. Retrieved from Project Muse database (doi:10.1353/scu.2013.0010).

   b. doi:10.1353/scu.2013.0010

Courtesy of Brookings Institution's Brown Center on Education Policy and author Tom Loveless; Photo: Reuters/Jim Young.

8. What is the correct APA reference list entry for this blog post on a website?

a. Loveless, T. (2013, April 3). *Ability grouping, tracking, and how schools work*. Retrieved from http://brookings.edu/blogs/brown-center-chalkboard/posts/2013/04/03-ability-grouping -tracking-loveless

b. Loveless, T. (2013, April 3). Ability grouping, tracking, and how schools work [Blog post]. Retrieved from http://www.brookings.edu/blogs/brown-center-chalkboard/posts/2013/04/ 03-ability-grouping-tracking-loveless

Hacker/Sommers, *Working with Sources: Exercises for Hacker Handbooks* (Boston: Bedford, 2018)

SOURCE: AN ARTICLE IN A MAGAZINE

Scientific American, table of contents page from *Scientific American* 292, no. 5 (May 2005): 6. Copyright © 2005 Scientific American, a division of Nature America, Inc. All rights reserved. This page includes images by Matt Collins, copyright © Matt Collins, reprinted by permission, and an image by Flynn Larsen, copyright © Flynn Larsen, reprinted by permission.

9. How would you cite the title of this article in an APA reference list entry?

   a. Insights: When medicine meets literature.

   b. When medicine meets literature.

10. What is the correct APA reference list entry for this source? (The article appears on pages 38 and 39 in the magazine.)

   a. Holloway, M. (2005, May). When medicine meets literature. *Scientific American, 292*(5), 38-39.

   b. Holloway, M. (2005). When medicine meets literature. *Scientific American, 292*(5), 38-39.

APA documentation: reference list 1

For help with this exercise, see the APA reference list section in your handbook.

Circle the letter of the APA reference list entry that is handled correctly.

EXAMPLE

The student has quoted from a fact sheet titled *Fracking in California: Questions and Concerns*, issued by the Climate Law Institute of the Center for Biological Diversity. The student accessed the fact sheet online at http://www.biologicaldiversity.org/action/toolbox/fracking/pdfs/CAFrackingFactsheet_May2013_2.pdf. It is undated.

(a.) Center for Biological Diversity, Climate Law Institute. (n.d.). *Fracking in California: Questions and concerns* [Fact sheet]. Retrieved from http://www.biologicaldiversity.org/action/toolbox/fracking/pdfs/CAFrackingFactsheet_May2013_2.pdf

b. Center for Biological Diversity, Climate Law Institute. *Fracking in California: Questions and concerns.* Retrieved from http://www.biologicaldiversity.org/action/toolbox/fracking/pdfs/CAFrackingFactsheet_May2013_2.pdf

1. The student has quoted from a 2012 article on the *Popular Mechanics* website, http://www.popularmechanics.com. The article, written by Seamus McGraw, is titled "Is Fracking Safe? The Top 10 Controversial Claims About Natural Gas Drilling." The complete URL is http://www.popularmechanics.com/science/energy/coal-oil-gas/top-10-myths-about-natural-gas-drilling-6386593#slide-1.

    a. McGraw, S. (2012). Is fracking safe? The top 10 controversial claims about natural gas drilling. *Popular Mechanics.* Retrieved from http://www.popularmechanics.com/

    b. McGraw, S. (2012). Is fracking safe? The top 10 controversial claims about natural gas drilling. *Popular Mechanics.* Retrieved from http://www.popularmechanics.com/science/energy/coal-oil-gas/top-10-myths-about-natural-gas-drilling-6386593#slide-1

2. The student has paraphrased information from a book titled *Fracking: America's Alternative Energy*, written by John Graves. The book was published in 2012 by Safe Harbor International Publishing, based in Ventura, California.

    a. Graves, J. (2012). *Fracking: America's alternative energy.* Ventura, CA: Safe Harbor International Publishing.

    b. Graves, J. (2012). *Fracking: America's Alternative Energy.* Ventura, CA: Safe Harbor International Publishing.

3. The student has summarized information from *Gasland*, a motion picture released in 2010, directed by Josh Fox. The student viewed the film via Netflix, at http://netflix.com/.

    a. Fox, J. (Director, 2010). *Gasland* [Video file]. Retrieved from Netflix at http://netflix.com/

    b. Fox, J. (Director). (2010). *Gasland* [Video file]. Retrieved from http://netflix.com/

4. The student has quoted from *Fracking: The Operations and Environmental Consequences of Hydraulic Fracturing*, a book by Michael D. Holloway and Oliver Rudd. The book was published in Beverly, Massachusetts, by Scrivener in 2013.

   a. Holloway, M. D., & Rudd, O. (2013). *Fracking: The operations and environmental consequences of hydraulic fracturing*. Beverly: Scrivener.

   b. Holloway, M. D., & Rudd, O. (2013). *Fracking: The operations and environmental consequences of hydraulic fracturing*. Beverly, MA: Scrivener.

5. The student has quoted from "The Whole Fracking Enchilada," an essay written by Sandra Steingraber and published on pages 315-318 of *The Best American Series: 20 Short Stories and Essays*. The book was published in 2012 in New York by Houghton Mifflin Harcourt. No editor is listed for the collection.

   a. Steingraber, S. (2012). The whole fracking enchilada. In (No Ed.), *The best American series: 20 short stories and essays* (pp. 315-318). New York, NY: Houghton Mifflin Harcourt.

   b. Steingraber, S. (2012). The whole fracking enchilada. In *The best American series: 20 short stories and essays* (pp. 315-318). New York, NY: Houghton Mifflin Harcourt.

6. The student has summarized information from an article in volume 477 of the scholarly journal *Nature*, published on September 15, 2011. The article, titled "Natural Gas: Should Fracking Stop?," was written by Robert W. Howarth, Anthony Ingraffea, and Terry Engelder and appeared on pages 271-275. The article has the DOI 10.1038/477271a.

   a. Howarth, R. W., Ingraffea, A., & Engelder, T. (2011). Natural gas: Should fracking stop? *Nature, 477,* 271-275. doi:10.1038/477271a

   b. Howarth, R. W., Ingraffea, A., & Engelder, T. (2011). Natural gas: Should fracking stop? *Nature, 477,* 271-275.

7. The student has cited data from the article "Mining: EPA Tackles Fracking" by John Manuel, published in May 2010 in volume 118 of *Environmental Health Perspectives*, an online journal. The URL for the article is http://ehp.niehs.nih.gov/118-a199/, and the journal's home page is http://ehp.niehs.nih.gov/.

   a. Manuel, J. (2010). Mining: EPA tackles fracking. *Environmental Health Perspectives, 118*. Retrieved from http://ehp.niehs.nih.gov/

   b. Manuel, J. (2010). Mining: EPA tackles fracking. *Environmental Health Perspectives, 118*. Retrieved from http://ehp.niehs.nih.gov/118-a199/

Hacker/Sommers, *Working with Sources: Exercises for Hacker Handbooks* (Boston: Bedford, 2018)

8. The student has quoted from a newspaper article by Danny Hakim. The article, "Gas Drilling Is Called Safe in New York," was published by *The New York Times* on January 3, 2012, and accessed online at http://www.nytimes.com/2013/01/03/nyregion/hydrofracking-safe-says-ny-health-dept-analysis .html?_r=0. The URL for the newspaper's home page is http://www.nytimes.com/.

   a. Hakim, D. (2012, January 3). Gas drilling is called safe in New York. *The New York Times*. Retrieved from http://www.nytimes.com/

   b. Hakim, D. (2012). Gas drilling is called safe in New York. *The New York Times*. Retrieved from http://www.nytimes.com/

9. The student has quoted from a radio report, "Environmentalists, Drillers Reach 'Truce' for Fracking Standards," by Elizabeth Shogren. The report appeared on the National Public Radio show *All Things Considered* on March 21, 2013, and the student accessed it on the NPR website, http://www.npr.org/.

   a. Shogren, E. (2013, March 21). Environmentalists, drillers reach "truce" for fracking standards [Radio series episode]. In *All Things Considered*. Retrieved from http://www.npr.org/

   b. Shogren, E. (2013, March 21). Environmentalists, drillers reach "truce" for fracking standards. *All Things Considered*. National Public Radio.

10. The student has cited Peter Aldhous's article "Drilling into the Unknown," which was published in the January 28, 2012, edition of the journal *New Scientist*. The article appeared on pages 8-10 of volume 213, and each issue of the journal begins with page 1. The student found the article through the Academic ASAP database, but the article does not have a DOI. The journal's home page is http://www.newscientist.com/.

    a. Aldhous, P. (2012). Drilling into the unknown. *New Scientist, 213*, 8-10. Retrieved from http://www .newscientist.com/

    b. Aldhous, P. (2012). Drilling into the unknown. *New Scientist, 213*, 8-10. Retrieved from Academic ASAP database.

APA documentation: reference list 2

For help with this exercise, see the APA reference list section in your handbook.

Circle the letter of the APA reference list entry that is handled correctly.

EXAMPLE

The student has summarized information from the article "Patterns of Parent-Reported Homework Problems among ADHD-referred and Non-referred Children." The article was written by Thomas J. Power, Branlyn E. Werba, Marley W. Watkins, Jennifer G. Angelucci, and Ricardo B. Eiraldi, and it appeared on pages 13-33 of volume 21, issue 1, of *School Psychology Quarterly* in 2006. The journal is paginated continuously throughout the volume.

a. Power, T. J., Werba, B. E., Watkins, M. W., Angelucci, J. G., & Eiraldi, R. B. (2006). Patterns of parent-reported homework problems among ADHD-referred and non-referred children. *School Psychology Quarterly, 21.*

b. Power, T. J., Werba, B. E., Watkins, M. W., Angelucci, J. G., & Eiraldi, R. B. (2006). Patterns of parent-reported homework problems among ADHD-referred and non-referred children. *School Psychology Quarterly, 21*, 13-33.

1. The student has summarized material from a government report titled *Teaching Children with Attention Deficit Hyperactivity Disorder: Instructional Strategies and Practices, 2008*, which was written and published in Washington, DC, in 2008 by the U.S. Department of Education.

   a. U.S. Department of Education. (2008). *Teaching children with attention deficit hyperactivity disorder: Instructional strategies and practices, 2008.* Washington, DC: Author.

   b. U.S. Department of Education. (2008). *Teaching children with attention deficit hyperactivity disorder: Instructional strategies and practices, 2008.* Washington, DC: U.S. Department of Education.

2. The student has quoted from an advertisement for the medication Concerta, which appears on pages 121-123 of the February 2009 issue of *O: The Oprah Magazine*. The volume number is 10, and the issue number is 2. The magazine is paginated by issue.

   a. Concerta [Medication]. (2009, February). *O: The Oprah Magazine, 10*(2), 121-123.

   b. Concerta [Advertisement]. (2009, February). *O: The Oprah Magazine, 10*(2), 121-123.

3. The student has paraphrased an article by Benedict Carey found on the website of *The New York Times* (http://nytimes.com/). The article title is "Early behavior therapy found to aid children with A.D.H.D." and is dated February 17, 2016.

   a. Carey, B. (2016, February 17). Early behavior therapy found to aid children with A.D.H.D. *The New York Times.* Retrieved from http://nytimes.com/

   b. Carey, B. (2016, February 17). Early behavior therapy found to aid children with A.D.H.D. *The New York Times.* Retrieved from *The New York Times* website.

4. The student has summarized material from an article in the journal *Developmental Psychology* titled "Gene x Environment Interactions in Reading Disability and Attention-Deficit/Hyperactivity Disorder." The article is in volume 45, issue 1, published in January 2009, and is printed on pages 77-89. The journal is paginated continuously throughout the volume. The authors are Bruce F. Pennington, Lauren M. McGrath, Jenni Rosenberg, Holly Barnard, Shelley D. Smith, Erik G. Willcutt, Angela Friend, John C. DeFries, and Richard K. Olson.

   a. Pennington, B. F., et al. (2009). Gene x environment interactions in reading disability and attention-deficit/hyperactivity disorder. *Developmental Psychology, 45*, 77-89.

   b. Pennington, B. F., McGrath, L. M., Rosenberg, J., Barnard, H., Smith, S. D., Willcutt, E. G., . . . Olson, R. K. (2009). Gene x environment interactions in reading disability and attention-deficit/hyperactivity disorder. *Developmental Psychology, 45*, 77-89.

5. The student has summarized information from pages 26-28 of the book *Teaching Young Children with ADHD: Successful Strategies and Practical Interventions for PreK-3,* by Richard A. Lougy, Silvia L. DeRuvo, and David Rosenthal. The book was published in Thousand Oaks, California, in 2007 by Corwin Press.

   a. Lougy, R. A., DeRuvo, S. L., & Rosenthal, D. (2007). *Teaching young children with ADHD: Successful strategies and practical interventions for preK-3.* Thousand Oaks, CA: Corwin Press, 26-28.

   b. Lougy, R. A., DeRuvo, S. L., & Rosenthal, D. (2007). *Teaching young children with ADHD: Successful strategies and practical interventions for preK-3.* Thousand Oaks, CA: Corwin Press.

6. The student has quoted material from a journal article accessed in the Academic OneFile database. The journal is *American Journal of Psychology*, and the article, "Implicit Theories of Intelligence, Perceived Academic Competence, and School Achievement: Testing Alternative Models," was published in volume 119, issue 2, in 2006, on pages 223-238. The journal is paginated continuously throughout the volume. The article was written by Eleftheria Gonida, Grigories Kiosseoglou, and Angeliki Leondari. The article has no DOI (digital object identifier). The database's accession number for the document is A147872672, and the writer found the journal's website at http://www.press.uillinois.edu/journals/ajp .html.

   a. Gonida, E., Kiosseoglou, G., & Leondari, A. (2006). Implicit theories of intelligence, perceived academic competence, and school achievement: Testing alternative models. *American Journal of Psychology, 119*, 223-238. Retrieved from http://www.press.uillinois.edu/journals/ajp.html

   b. Gonida, E., Kiosseoglou, G., & Leondari, A. (2006). Implicit theories of intelligence, perceived academic competence, and school achievement: Testing alternative models. *American Journal of Psychology, 119*, 223-238. Retrieved from Academic OneFile database. (A147872672)

Hacker/Sommers, *Working with Sources: Exercises for Hacker Handbooks* (Boston: Bedford, 2018)

7. The student has paraphrased material from an article titled "Structural and Functional Brain Abnormalities in Attention-Deficit/Hyperactivity Disorder and Obsessive-Compulsive Disorder," published on August 1, 2016, in a scholarly journal, *Journal of the American Medical Association Psychiatry*, volume 73, issue 8, pages 815-825. The journal is paginated continuously throughout the volume. The article was written by Luke J. Norman, Christina Carlisi, and Steve Lukito.

   a. Norman, L. J., Carlisi, C., & Lukito, S. (2016). Structural and functional brain abnormalities in attention-deficit/hyperactivity disorder and obsessive-compulsive disorder. *Journal of the American Medical Association Psychiatry, 73,* 815-825.

   b. Norman, L. J., Carlisi, C., & Lukito, S. (2016, August 1). Structural and functional brain abnormalities in attention-deficit/hyperactivity disorder and obsessive-compulsive disorder. *Journal of the American Medical Association Psychiatry, 73,* 815-825.

8. The student summarized information from a podcast that was retrieved from the website http://www.pbs.org/merrow/podcast/. The podcast is called "The Right Answer?" from the series *Education Podcast with John Merrow*. It was produced by Jane Renaud, and there is no date of posting.

   a. Renaud, J. (Producer). (n.d.). The right answer? [Audio podcast]. *Education podcast with John Merrow.* Retrieved from http://www.pbs.org/merrow/podcast/

   b. Renaud, J. (Producer). (n.d.). The right answer? *Education podcast with John Merrow.* Retrieved from http://www.pbs.org/merrow/podcast/

9. The student has quoted from an online video file titled "How to Treat ADHD in Children," hosted by Matthew H. Erdelyi. No date is given for the video online; it was accessed by the student on January 30, 2009. The URL is http://www.articlesbase.com/videos/5min/29158215.

   a. Erdelyi, M. H. (Host). (2009, 30 January). How to treat ADHD in children [Video file]. Retrieved from http://www.articlesbase.com/videos/5min/29158215

   b. Erdelyi, M. H. (Host). (n.d.). How to treat ADHD in children [Video file]. Retrieved from http://www.articlesbase.com/videos/5min/29158215

10. The student has quoted material from an interview titled "What's New with ADHD?" The interview was conducted by Richard L. Peck and was published in volume 26, issue 1 of *Behavioral Health Management* in 2001. The interview was with E. Clarke Ross and appears on pages 26-30 of the journal. The journal is paginated by issue.

   a. Peck, R. L. (2001). What's new with ADHD? [Interview with E. C. Ross]. *Behavioral Health Management, 26*(1), 26-30.

   b. Ross, E. C. (2001). What's new with ADHD? [Interview by R. L. Peck]. *Behavioral Health Management, 26*(1), 26-30.

APA documentation: reference list 3

For help with this exercise, see the APA reference list section in your handbook.

Circle the letter of the APA reference list entry that is handled correctly.

EXAMPLE

The student has summarized information from the book *The Longevity Revolution: The Benefits and Challenges of Living a Long Life*, by Robert N. Butler. The book was published in New York in 2008 by PublicAffairs.

a. Butler, R. N. *The longevity revolution: The benefits and challenges of living a long life.* New York, NY: PublicAffairs, 2008.

(b.) Butler, R. N. (2008). *The longevity revolution: The benefits and challenges of living a long life.* New York, NY: PublicAffairs.

1. The student has summarized material from a document titled "Inside the Brain: An Interactive Tour" on the Alzheimer's Association website. The copyright date for the article is 2008, and there is no named author. The URL is http://www.alz.org/alzheimers_disease_4719.asp.

   a. *Inside the brain: An interactive tour.* (2008). Retrieved from http://www.alz.org/alzheimers _disease_4719.asp

   b. Alzheimer's Association. (2008). *Inside the brain: An interactive tour.* Retrieved from http://www.alz .org/alzheimers_disease_4719.asp

2. The student has quoted from a documentary DVD titled *The Forgetting: A Portrait of Alzheimer's*, dated 2004. Elizabeth Arledge is listed as the producer and director, and Warner Home Video, in Burbank, California, is the distributor.

   a. Arledge, E., Producer/director. (2004). *The forgetting: A portrait of Alzheimer's* [DVD]. Burbank, CA: Warner Home Video.

   b. Arledge, E. (Producer/director). (2004). *The forgetting: A portrait of Alzheimer's* [DVD]. Burbank, CA: Warner Home Video.

3. The student has paraphrased an article by Joseph Nocera, "Taking Science Personally," found on page F1 in *The New York Times*, November 11, 2008.

   a. Nocera, J. (2008, November 11). Taking science personally. *The New York Times*, p. F1.

   b. Nocera, J. (2008, November 11). Taking science personally. *The New York Times*, F1.

4. The student has quoted material from page 320 of an article in volume 43, issue 3 of the *British Journal of Clinical Psychology*. The article, "Life Events, Depression, and Social Support in Dementia," was published in September 2004 and is printed on pages 313-324. The journal is paginated continuously throughout the volume. The authors are Allyson Waite, Paul Bebbington, Martin Skelton-Robinson, and Martin Orrell.

    a. Waite, A., Bebbington, P., Skelton-Robinson, M., & Orrell, M. (2004). Life events, depression, and social support in dementia. *British Journal of Clinical Psychology*, *43*, 313-324.

    b. Waite, A., Bebbington, P., Skelton-Robinson, M., & Orrell, M. (2004). Life events, depression, and social support in dementia. *British Journal of Clinical Psychology*, *43*, 320.

5. The student has summarized information from the book *Aging, Biotechnology, and the Future*, edited by Catherine Y. Read, Robert C. Green, and Michael A. Smyer. The book was published in Baltimore, Maryland, in 2008 by Johns Hopkins University Press.

    a. Read, C. Y., Green, R. C., & Smyer, M. A. (Eds.). (2008). *Aging, biotechnology, and the future.* Baltimore, MD: Johns Hopkins University Press.

    b. Read, C. Y., Green, R. C., & Smyer, M. A. (2008). *Aging, biotechnology, and the future.* Baltimore, MD: Johns Hopkins University Press.

6. The student has quoted material from an article, "Behavioral Medicine and Aging," in the *Journal of Consulting and Clinical Psychology*, accessed in the PsycARTICLES database. The article was published in volume 70, issue 3 in June 2002, on pages 843-851. The journal is paginated continuously throughout the volume. The article was written by Ilene C. Siegler, Lori A. Bastian, David C. Steffens, Hayden B. Bosworth, and Paul T. Costa. The database provides the DOI (digital object identifier) 10.1037/0022-006X.70.3.843 for the article.

    a. Siegler, I. C., Bastian, L. A., Steffens, D. C., Bosworth, H. B., & Costa, P. T. (2002). Behavioral medicine and aging. *Journal of Consulting and Clinical Psychology*, *70*, 843-851. Retrieved from PsycARTICLES database. doi:10.1037/0022-006X.70.3.843

    b. Siegler, I. C., Bastian, L. A., Steffens, D. C., Bosworth, H. B., & Costa, P. T. (2002). Behavioral medicine and aging. *Journal of Consulting and Clinical Psychology*, *70*, 843-851. doi:10.1037/0022-006X.70.3.843

7. The student has paraphrased material from an article titled "The Role of Coping Humor in the Physical and Mental Health of Older Adults," published in November 2008 in the scholarly journal *Aging and Mental Health*, volume 12, issue 6, pages 713-718. The journal is paginated continuously throughout the volume. The article was written by Elsa Marziali, Lynn McDonald, and Peter Donahue.

    a. Marziali, E., McDonald, L., & Donahue, P. (2008). The role of coping humor in the physical and mental health of older adults. *Aging and Mental Health*, *12*, 713-718.

    b. Marziali, E., McDonald, L., & Donahue, P. (2008, November). The role of coping humor in the physical and mental health of older adults. *Aging and Mental Health*, *12*, 713-718.

8. The student summarized information from an audio file that was retrieved from the website http://www.npr.org/templates/story/story.php?storyId=99958952. The story, "Brain Study Indicates Why Some Memories Persist," was reported by Jon Hamilton and posted on January 29, 2009. The student retrieved the story on February 8, 2009.

   a. Hamilton, J. (2008, January 29). Brain study indicates why some memories persist [Audio file]. Retrieved February 8, 2009, from http://www.npr.org/templates/story/story.php?storyId=99958952

   b. Hamilton, J. (2008, January 29). Brain study indicates why some memories persist [Audio file]. Retrieved from http://www.npr.org/templates/story/story.php?storyId=99958952

9. The student has paraphrased information from an abstract of a journal article titled "Aging and Emotional Memory: Cognitive Mechanisms Underlying the Positivity Effect." The article was written by Julia Spaniol, Andreas Voss, and Cheryl L. Grady and appears on pages 859-872 of volume 23, issue 4 of *Psychology and Aging*, published in December 2008. The journal is paginated continuously throughout the volume.

   a. Spaniol, J., Voss, A., & Grady, C. L. (2008). Abstract of Aging and emotional memory: Cognitive mechanisms underlying the positivity effect. *Psychology and Aging, 23*, 859-872.

   b. Spaniol, J., Voss, A., & Grady, C. L. (2008). Aging and emotional memory: Cognitive mechanisms underlying the positivity effect [Abstract]. *Psychology and Aging, 23*, 859-872.

10. The student is quoting material from a doctoral dissertation by Lea Angela Truman Drye titled *Examining the Relationship of Education and Late-Life Mental Activity with Cognitive Decline*, dated 2008. The dissertation was retrieved from the ProQuest Dissertations and Theses database and has the accession number AAT 3309643.

    a. Drye, L. A. T. (2008). *Examining the relationship of education and late-life mental activity with cognitive decline* (Doctoral dissertation). Available from ProQuest Dissertations and Theses database. (AAT 3309643)

    b. Drye, L. A. T. (2008). *Examining the relationship of education and late-life mental activity with cognitive decline.* Available from ProQuest Dissertations and Theses database.

APA documentation

For help with this exercise, see the section on APA documentation in your handbook.

Write "true" if the statement is true or "false" if it is false.

1. A page number is required for all APA in-text citations.

2. In the text of a paper, the author(s) of a source and the source's date must be given either in a signal phrase introducing the cited material or in parentheses following it.

3. The list of references is organized alphabetically by authors' last names (or by title for a work with no author).

4. When citing a source with two authors in the text of the paper, use an ampersand (&) to join the names either in a signal phrase introducing the source or in parentheses at the end of the citation.

5. When you include a page number or numbers in parentheses at the end of a citation, precede the number or numbers with the abbreviation "p." or "pp."

6. APA style recommends using the present tense in a signal phrase introducing cited material (for example, "Baker reports that" or "Wu argues that").

7. When a paper cites two or more works by an author published in the same year, each work is assigned a lowercase letter, beginning with "a" and based on the alphabetical order of the works' titles. The letter appears after the year of publication in both in-text citations and the list of references.

8. If available, a date is supplied for all in-text citations; if no date is available, the abbreviation "n.d." is used instead.

9. If a work has eight or more authors, use the first author's name followed by "et al." in the reference list.

10. For a work with an unknown author, give the work's full title and its date in a signal phrase introducing the source or use a brief title and the date in parentheses following the source. Name "Anonymous" as the author only if the work specifies "Anonymous" as the author.

Hacker/Sommers, *Working with Sources: Exercises for Hacker Handbooks* (Boston: Bedford, 2018)

Thesis statements in *Chicago* (CMS) papers 1

For help with this exercise, see the section on thesis statements in *Chicago* (CMS) papers in your handbook.

Circle the letter of the sentence in each pair that would work well as the thesis statement for a research paper from five to ten pages long. Remember that a thesis should be a central idea that requires supporting evidence; it should be of adequate scope for a five-to-ten-page paper; and it should be sharply focused.

EXAMPLE

a. Although Jean Jacques Dessalines, commander of the revolutionary forces in Haiti, encouraged his soldiers to commit atrocities, his tactics may have been necessary to ensure that slavery would not return to Haiti.

b. After winning independence for Haiti and expelling people of European ancestry from the country, military leader Jean Jacques Dessalines declared himself emperor for life in 1804.

1. a. The development of general anesthesia made modern surgery possible, for it allowed surgeons to work slowly and carefully for the first time.

   b. On October 16, 1846, observers of the first surgery performed on a person anesthetized with ether were astonished when the patient neither screamed nor seemed aware of any pain.

2. a. A surprising number of adventurers who achieved fame as explorers were later revealed to be charlatans who had not even found the places they said they had discovered.

   b. Robert E. Peary is still credited by many people with the discovery of the North Pole in 1909, but the available evidence strongly suggests that he never reached his goal.

3. a. Many old Hollywood films have disappeared forever as the single surviving copies disintegrate from exposure to heat and moisture.

   b. Because old Hollywood films capture historical moments that would otherwise be lost, restoring and preserving at least one copy of every possible film is a task that American scholars should support.

4. a. The electoral college, which was created in the eighteenth century to solve the problem of voters' lack of knowledge about candidates from other states, never worked as the framers of the Constitution intended.

   b. The electoral college system was developed in the eighteenth century under circumstances much different from those facing the country today.

5. a. The United States caused needless civilian casualties by dropping an atomic bomb on Nagasaki in 1945, for the bombing of Hiroshima had already convinced the Japanese authorities to surrender.

   b. Nagasaki, a populous Japanese city on an inlet of the East China Sea, was devastated on August 9, 1945, by the second atomic bomb dropped by the United States.

6. a. Evidence from the trial of Bridget Bishop, the first woman hanged for practicing witchcraft in Salem, Massachusetts, indicates that Bishop had indeed been attempting to cast spells.

   b. For centuries in much of Europe, women who were midwives or herbalists were often charged with practicing magic because they were regarded with deep suspicion by Christian clergymen.

7. a. The British, who are famous for their love of horses, used horses in warfare even when modern equipment, such as tanks, became an available option.

   b. The extended carnage in the trenches of the western front in World War I could have been ended much sooner if British military officers had been willing to use tanks instead of horses in battle.

8. a. Israel has been struggling against one enemy or another since the United Nations voted to establish the Jewish state in 1948.

   b. Citizens of Arab countries have long been encouraged to express grievances against Israel, while they are seldom permitted to speak out against oppressive policies of their own governments; this deflected anger has contributed to the vehemence of anti-Israeli feeling in many Arab lands.

9. a. To the surprise of modern scholars, the ancient Greek explanation for the prophetic powers of the oracle at Delphi—fumes that rose from the floor of the Temple of Apollo—may have a basis in fact, for the temple sits above the intersection of two underground faults that allow fumes of the hallucinogen ethylene to percolate up through the underlying limestone.

   b. For more than twelve centuries, ancient Greeks traveled to the Temple of Apollo at Delphi to consult the oracle there, and they believed that the prophecies she made while in a trance were divinely inspired.

10. a. For decades, great buildings have been demolished in this country—from coast to coast and in cities and towns—because Americans have little sense of history.

    b. The demolition of New York's Penn Station was the catalyst for the creation of the New York City Landmarks Preservation Commission, which helped save and restore other landmarks, including Grand Central Station and the New York Public Library.

Hacker/Sommers, *Working with Sources: Exercises for Hacker Handbooks* (Boston: Bedford, 2018)

Thesis statements in *Chicago* (CMS) papers 2

For help with this exercise, see the section on thesis statements in *Chicago* (CMS) papers in your handbook.

Circle the letter of the sentence in each pair that would work well as the thesis statement for a research paper from five to ten pages long. Remember that a thesis should be a central idea that requires supporting evidence; it should be of adequate scope for a five-to-ten-page paper; and it should be sharply focused.

EXAMPLE

a. Mohandas Gandhi was the leader of the Indian movement for independence from Britain.

(b.) Mohandas Gandhi was a successful political leader in large part because of his commitment to nonviolence during India's struggle for independence.

1. a. Ever since President John F. Kennedy was shot to death in November 1963, people have wondered whether his assassin, Lee Harvey Oswald, was working alone or as part of a conspiracy.

   b. The tragic circumstances surrounding President John F. Kennedy's death in 1963 were instrumental in allowing Lyndon B. Johnson to achieve many of his Great Society initiatives.

2. a. Lord Elgin removed friezes from the Parthenon and housed them in the British Museum in the early nineteenth century, thus earning them the name "Elgin marbles."

   b. The British Museum should honor Greece's request to have the ancient Parthenon friezes, known as the Elgin marbles, returned to their native country and displayed in a Greek museum.

3. a. Richard Nixon was probably not the first president to engage in illegal activity while in office, but Americans in 1973, war-weary and distrustful of authority, would no longer tolerate excuses based on historical precedent.

   b. Throughout history, presidents have been suspected of engaging in illegal activity, but few have been involved in scandals that caught the attention of the public, and even fewer have been impeached.

4. a. In the decades following World War II, many Americans began to realize the extent of the Japanese internment in the early 1940s.

   b. In the second half of the twentieth century, Americans were able to accept responsibility for the mistakes made during the Japanese internment of World War II largely because Japan was no longer seen as a military threat.

5. a. The most successful Jesuit missionaries in China during the Ming dynasty were able to adapt to Chinese culture: learning Mandarin, adopting Chinese clothing, and finding parallels between Christianity and the teachings of Confucius.

    b. Throughout history, the most successful missionaries have been those willing to engage in diplomacy with the people of power, respect the customs and language of the people they served, and emphasize similarities rather than differences between traditions.

6. a. Within two decades of their arrival in Peru, the Spanish nuns founded a convent in Cuzco called Santa Clara, which was given control over much of the confiscated Inca lands.

    b. Much of the economic power in colonial Peru was held by cloistered nuns, who played a crucial role in that country's early development.

7. a. In 1921, the long-term goal of the Chinese Communist Party was to form a Communist society, but it first focused on organizing the working class and on removing foreign influence from the government.

    b. Although not all historians agree, evidence suggests that the success of the Chinese Communist Party was due in large part to the Japanese invasions of Manchuria and central China in the 1930s.

8. a. Concern about a growing threat from Nazi Germany was the principal reason that the United States did not adequately prepare for a possible Japanese attack on Pearl Harbor.

    b. There is no way of knowing why the United States was so unprepared for the surprise Japanese attack on Pearl Harbor on December 7, 1941.

9. a. The United Nations had to weigh many competing agendas when it created the Jewish state of Israel in 1948.

    b. The British withdrawal from Palestine in 1947 had more to do with Britain's economic and political motives at home than with its relations with other countries.

10. a. In May 1966, Protestant loyalists in Northern Ireland formed the Ulster Volunteer Force, a paramilitary group whose aim was to combat the Irish Republican Army.

    b. Evidence suggests that protests in Northern Ireland against Catholic discrimination in the 1960s were heavily influenced by the American civil rights movement.

Hacker/Sommers, *Working with Sources: Exercises for Hacker Handbooks* (Boston: Bedford, 2018)

Avoiding plagiarism in *Chicago* (CMS) papers 1

For help with this exercise, see the section on avoiding plagiarism in *Chicago* (CMS) papers in your handbook.

Read the following passage and the information about its source. Then decide whether each student sample is plagiarized or uses the source correctly. If the student sample is plagiarized, write "plagiarized"; if the sample is acceptable, write "OK."

ORIGINAL SOURCE

Unaccountable power always breeds resentment, especially when it is money power. The Rothschilds were demonized in Europe in much the same way as J. P. Morgan was in the United States—only more so, because they were Jewish. The myth of their omnipotence, in which they themselves sometimes believed, bred a virulent anti-Semitism, which fastened onto a uniquely visible Jewish family. To conservatives the Rothschilds were a standing threat to the established hierarchy; to socialists they stood for unbridled exploitation of the worker. Long after their power had disappeared, Hitler combined the two strands into a lethal cocktail, when he referred to the "rapacity of a Rothschild, who financed war and revolutions and brought the peoples into interest-servitude through loans." The origins of Auschwitz can be traced in part to this fateful coupling.

From Skidelsky, Robert. "Family Values." Review of *The House of Rothschild: The World's Banker, 1849-1999* and *The House of Rothschild: Money's Prophets*, 1789-1848, both by Niall Ferguson. *New York Review of Books*, December 16, 1999, 24-29. [The source passage is from page 24.]

1. According to Robert Skidelsky, members of the Rothschild family were demonized in Europe much as J. P. Morgan was in the United States—only more so due to the fact that they were Jewish.[1]

2. Historian Robert Skidelsky notes, "The Rothschilds were demonized in Europe in much the same way as J. P. Morgan was in the United States—only more so, because they were Jewish."[2]

3. Robert Skidelsky observes that the Rothschild family earned particular enmity not only for being tremendously wealthy and powerful but also for being Jewish.[3]

4. Robert Skidelsky says of the Rothschilds that the myth of their omnipotence bred a virulent anti-Semitism, which fastened onto a uniquely visible Jewish family.[4]

5. To conservatives the Rothschilds were a standing threat to the established hierarchy; to socialists they stood for unbridled exploitation of the worker.

6. After the Rothschild family no longer wielded power, Robert Skidelsky writes, Hitler used both conservatives' and socialists' negative views of that wealthy family to incite hatred of the Jews.[5]

7. In the view of Robert Skidelsky, Hitler used both conservatives' and socialists' negative opinions of the wealthy Rothschild family and the power they had once wielded to incite hatred of the Jews.[6]

8. Robert Skidelsky points out the Rothschild family's place in Hitler's demonization of the Jews, noting that Hitler combined the two strands of the conservatives' and socialists' hatred of the Rothschilds into a lethal cocktail.

9. Robert Skidelsky points out the Rothschild family's place in Hitler's demonization of the Jews, noting that Hitler "combined the two strands" of the conservatives' and the socialists' hatred of the Rothschilds to incite anti-Semitism.[7]

10. According to Robert Skidelsky, the beginnings of the concentration camps can be seen in part in the momentous combination of the conservatives' and the socialists' hatred of the Rothschilds.[8]

Hacker/Sommers, *Working with Sources: Exercises for Hacker Handbooks* (Boston: Bedford, 2018)

Avoiding plagiarism in *Chicago* (CMS) papers 2

For help with this exercise, see the section on avoiding plagiarism in *Chicago* (CMS) papers in your handbook.

Read the following passage and the information about its source. Then decide whether each student sample is plagiarized or uses the source correctly. If the student sample is plagiarized, write "plagiarized"; if the sample is acceptable, write "OK."

ORIGINAL SOURCE

Years after the battle [Battle of the Little Bighorn] a number of Indians claimed that the soldiers became so terrified they dropped their guns. In fact, quite a few did drop their guns or throw them aside, although not necessarily in panic. The guns occasionally jammed because the soft copper shells—unlike hard brass—could be deformed by exploding powder, causing them to stick in the breech. Furthermore, troopers often carried loose ammunition in saddlebags where it was easily damaged. Another possible reason turned up when one of [Major] Reno's men talked with an ordnance officer. This officer subsequently wrote to the Chief of Ordnance that Custer's troops used ammunition belts made from scrap leather. The copper shells "thus had become covered with a coating of verdigris and extraneous matter, which had made it difficult to even put them in the chamber before the gun had been discharged at all. Upon discharge the verdigris and extraneous matter formed a cement which held the sides of the cartridge in place against the action of the ejector. . . ."

Whatever the cause, it could take some time to pry a deformed shell out of the breech, or one that had been cemented in place, which explains why troopers under attack occasionally threw aside their rifles. To the Indians it must have appeared that a soldier who did this was terrified—as of course he might have been—but at the same time he might have been enraged.

From Connell, Evan S. *Son of the Morning Star: Custer and the Little Bighorn*. San Francisco: North Point Press, 1984. [The source passage is from pages 306-7.]

1. Evan S. Connell admits that many soldiers at the Battle of the Little Bighorn "did drop their guns or throw them aside" but argues that they did so "not necessarily in panic."[1]

2. According to Evan S. Connell, a number of Indians claimed that the soldiers at the Battle of the Little Bighorn were so frightened they dropped their weapons.[2]

3. As Evan S. Connell notes, the soldiers' guns at the Battle of the Little Bighorn might have jammed because the soft copper shells could be deformed by exploding powder, causing them to stick in the breech.[3]

4. Accepting the testimony that some soldiers at the Battle of the Little Bighorn abandoned their weapons, Evan S. Connell explains that the bullets had a disastrous tendency to stick in the soldiers' guns.[4]

5. Evan S. Connell points out that the weapons occasionally failed to fire because the pliant copper bullets—as opposed to hard brass—had been bent out of shape by detonating gunpowder, making them jam in the breech; in addition, loose ammunition was often toted in saddlebags where it was easily deformed.[5]

6. Imagining Custer's men struggling to pry bullets out of their jammed guns in the heat of the Battle of the Little Bighorn, Evan S. Connell convincingly argues that while the soldiers might indeed have been frenzied with fear, those who decided to abandon their weapons probably did not act out of irrational panic.[6]

7. Evan S. Connell explains that in a letter to the Chief of Ordnance, an officer reported that Custer's troops used ammunition belts made from scrap leather and suggested that residue from the leather could have caused some shells to jam.[7]

8. An officer under the command of Reno reported that the soldiers' leather ammunition belts coated the shells with a substance that sometimes made the guns jam, according to Evan S. Connell.[8]

9. When the guns jammed, Evan S. Connell notes, it could take some time to pry a deformed shell out of the breech, or one that had been cemented in place, which explains why troopers under attack occasionally threw aside their rifles.

10. "To the Indians," Evan S. Connell writes, "it must have appeared that a soldier who [threw aside his rifle] was terrified—as of course he might have been—but at the same time he might have been enraged."[9]

Hacker/Sommers, *Working with Sources: Exercises for Hacker Handbooks* (Boston: Bedford, 2018)

Avoiding plagiarism in *Chicago* (CMS) papers 3

For help with this exercise, see the section on avoiding plagiarism in *Chicago* (CMS) papers in your handbook.

Read the following passage and the information about its source. Then decide whether each student sample is plagiarized or uses the source correctly. If the student sample is plagiarized, write "plagiarized"; if the sample is acceptable, write "OK."

ORIGINAL SOURCE

From the beginning, Nome [a city in Alaska] depended on its dogs. Teams were drafted into service as mail trucks, ambulances, freight trains, and long-distance taxis. The demand for sled dogs was so high, particularly during the northern gold rushes, that the supply of dogs ran out and a black market for the animals sprang up in the states. Any dog that looked as if it could pull a sled or carry a saddlebag—whether or not it was suited to withstand the cold—was kidnapped and sold in the north. "It was said at the time that no dog larger than a spaniel was considered safe on the streets" of West Coast port towns, said one sled dog historian.

From Salisbury, Gay, and Laney Salisbury. *The Cruelest Miles: The Heroic Story of Dogs and Men in a Race against an Epidemic.* New York: Norton, 2003. [The source passage is from page 20.]

1. According to Salisbury and Salisbury, so many people in Alaska wanted sled dogs during the gold rush period that large dogs were stolen from the United States and sold illegally in Alaska.[1]

2. Salisbury and Salisbury explain that the city of Nome, Alaska, depended on its dogs from the beginning of its existence.[2]

3. In Nome, as Salisbury and Salisbury point out, dogsleds acted as freight trains, mail trucks, taxis, and ambulances.[3]

4. Salisbury and Salisbury note that in Alaska during the gold rush, there were so many uses for sled dogs "that the supply of dogs ran out and a black market for the animals sprang up in the states."[4]

5. Every canine that appeared able to haul a dogsled or bear a pack on its back, notwithstanding its ability to deal with winter weather, was taken secretly and marketed in Alaska, say Salisbury and Salisbury.[5]

Avoiding plagiarism in *Chicago* (CMS) papers 4

For help with this exercise, see the section on avoiding plagiarism in *Chicago* (CMS) papers in your handbook.

Read the following passage and the information about its source. Then decide whether each student sample is plagiarized or uses the source correctly. If the student sample is plagiarized, write "plagiarized"; if the sample is acceptable, write "OK."

ORIGINAL SOURCE

When Claudius died in October 54, at the age of sixty-three, there were several divergent accounts of what had caused his death. But according to the version which subsequently prevailed most widely, [his wife] Agrippina had killed him with poisoned mushrooms. This must be regarded as likely though not quite certain, since accidental loss of life frequently occurs in Italy owing to confusions between the harmless mushroom *boletus edulis* and the fatal *amanita phalloides*. Besides Agrippina had cleared the ground adequately for [her son] Nero's succession, and only had to wait. But perhaps that was just what she dared not do, because if Nero, who was nearly seventeen, did not come to the throne fairly soon, he might no longer be young enough to need her as his effective regent.

From Grant, Michael. *The Twelve Caesars*. New York: Scribner's, 1975. [The source passage is from page 147.]

1. The most likely but not quite certain cause of Claudius's death, says Grant, was that his wife had killed him with poisoned mushrooms.[1]

2. To bolster the view that Claudius might have eaten poisoned mushrooms accidentally, Grant notes that many people in Italy still die when they mistake an edible mushroom for a similar-looking but deadly one.[2]

3. According to Grant, there was no single predominant story but rather "several divergent accounts" of how Claudius died.[3]

4. Grant argues that Agrippina had prepared the way successfully for her son's eventual succession and needed only to bide her time until Nero would be emperor, with her acting as regent.[4]

5. Grant speculates that Agrippina could not wait for Claudius to die naturally because her son, Claudius's successor, would soon be old enough to rule on his own and would not need his mother as regent.[5]

Hacker/Sommers, *Working with Sources: Exercises for Hacker Handbooks* (Boston: Bedford, 2018)

Recognizing common knowledge in *Chicago* (CMS) papers

For help with this exercise, see the section on recognizing common knowledge in *Chicago* (CMS) papers in your handbook.

Read the student passage and determine whether the student needs to cite the source of the information in a *Chicago* (CMS) paper. If the material does not need citation because it is common knowledge, write "common knowledge." If the material is not common knowledge and the student should cite the source, write "needs citation."

EXAMPLE

Small's Paradise, one of the most famous nightclubs of the Harlem Renaissance, was the only well-known New York nightclub of the era owned by an African American. **Needs citation** [This very specific fact about a little-known establishment requires citation. In addition, the statement that the nightclub was the *only* one owned by an African American must be supported by a source.]

1. In Rwanda in 1994, a civil war left hundreds of thousands of Tutsis and moderate Hutus dead.

2. Tong wars erupted in New York's Chinatown in the early decades of the twentieth century, giving that neighborhood the city's highest murder rate.

3. Abraham Lincoln was assassinated in Ford's Theatre in Washington, DC, as he sat watching a play.

4. After the Civil War, forty thousand former slaves had successful farms on the Sea Islands of South Carolina—the only place in the South where African Americans owned sizable quantities of land.

5. The eruption of a volcano on the island of Krakatau in Indonesia in 1883 spewed dense volcanic dust high into the atmosphere, blocking sunlight and lowering temperatures worldwide for months.

6. The US invasion of Cambodia in 1970 led to antiwar protests on many college campuses.

7. A Sherpa named Tenzing Norgay helped guide Edmund Hillary to the top of Mount Everest in 1953.

8. General George Custer and all of his men were killed at the Battle of the Little Bighorn.

9. The underground railroad provided shelter, guides, and assistance to runaway slaves as they made their way north to freedom.

10. Beginning in March 1988 and continuing for seventeen months, Saddam Hussein had his air force drop poison gas on more than two hundred Kurdish villages and towns in Iraq.

Integrating sources in *Chicago* (CMS) papers 1

For help with this exercise, see the section on integrating sources in *Chicago* (CMS) papers in your handbook.

Read the following passage and the information about its source. Then decide whether each student sample uses the source correctly. If the student has made an error in using the source, revise the sample to avoid the error. If the student has quoted correctly, write "OK."

ORIGINAL SOURCE

Practices associated with normal births in medieval Europe are shrouded in secrecy, not because the births were hidden at the time, but because they were a woman's ritual and women did not pass on information about them in writing. Indeed, we can be quite sure that the event of a birth was well known within the immediate community. Living close together, the neighbors would hear the cries of a woman in labor and would observe the midwife and female friends gathering around. But what occurred in the birthing chamber was not known to the men listening outside, and so it was not recorded. The learned clerical treatises on gynecology contain no descriptions of normal births, only abnormal ones. Male doctors never attended a normal birth, so they knew nothing about them. They were called in only when surgery was needed.

From Hanawalt, Barbara A. *Growing Up in Medieval London*. Oxford: Oxford University Press, 1993. [The source passage is from page 42.]

1. Barbara Hanawalt observes that little is known about how women gave birth in medieval Europe "not because the births were hidden at the time, but because they were a woman's ritual and women did not pass on information about them in writing."[1]

2. According to Barbara Hanawalt, "Practices associated with normal births in medieval Europe were secret."[2]

3. Although women in the Middle Ages, like women throughout history, had children, little is known about procedures related to ordinary births. "Practices associated with normal births in medieval Europe are shrouded in secrecy, not because the births were hidden at the time, but because they were a woman's ritual and women did not pass on information about them in writing."[3]

4. Barbara Hanawalt points out that neighbors would certainly have known when a birth was imminent because they "would hear the cries of a woman in labor and would observe the midwife and female friends gathering around."[4]

5. Barbara Hanawalt notes that because "what occurred in the birthing chamber was not known to the men . . . it was not recorded."[5]

6. According to Barbara Hanawalt,

   "Practices associated with normal births in medieval Europe are shrouded in secrecy, not because the births were hidden at the time, but because they were a woman's ritual and women did not pass on information about them in writing. Indeed, we can be quite sure that the event of a birth was well known within the immediate community. Living close together, the neighbors would hear the cries of a woman in labor and would observe the midwife and female friends gathering around. But what occurred in the birthing chamber was not known to the men listening outside, and so it was not recorded."[6]

7. Little is known today about normal births in the Middle Ages. Barbara Hanawalt explains that births "were a woman's ritual and women did not pass on information about them in writing. But what occurred in the birthing chamber was not known to the men listening outside, and so it was not recorded."[7]

8. Barbara Hanawalt notes, "[Medieval] learned clerical treatises on gynecology contain no descriptions of normal births, only abnormal ones. Male doctors never attended a normal birth, so they knew nothing about them. They were called in only when surgery was needed."[8]

9. Only abnormal births are described in learned medieval writings. "Male doctors never attended a normal birth, so they knew nothing about them. They were called in only when surgery was needed."[9]

10. Barbara Hanawalt observes that historians know little about normal childbirths in medieval times because childbirths were witnessed only by women, " and women did not pass on information about them in writing."[10]

Hacker/Sommers, *Working with Sources: Exercises for Hacker Handbooks* (Boston: Bedford, 2018)

Integrating sources in *Chicago* (CMS) papers 2

For help with this exercise, see the section on integrating sources in *Chicago* (CMS) papers in your handbook.

Read the following passage and the information about its source. Then decide whether each student sample uses the source correctly. If the student has made an error in using the source, revise the sample to avoid the error. If the student has quoted correctly, write "OK."

ORIGINAL SOURCE

Conflicts such as the seven major Anglo-French wars fought between 1689 and 1815 were struggles of endurance. Victory therefore went to the Power—or better, since both Britain and France usually had allies, to the Great Power coalition—with the greater capacity to maintain credit and to keep on raising supplies. The mere fact that these were *coalition* wars increased their duration, since a belligerent whose resources were fading would look to a more powerful ally for loans and reinforcements in order to keep itself in the fight. Given such expensive and exhausting conflicts, what each side desperately required was—to use the old aphorism—"money, money, and yet more money."

From Kennedy, Paul. *The Rise and Fall of the Great Powers: Economic Change and Military Conflict from 1500 to 2000.* New York: Random House, 1987. [The source passage is from page 76.]

1. Kennedy refers to the seven wars between Britain and France from 1689 to 1815 as "struggles of endurance."[1]

2. In the Anglo-French wars prior to 1815, "victory . . . went to the Power—or better, since both Britain and France usually had allies, to the Great Power coalition—with the greater capacity to maintain credit and to keep on raising supplies."[2]

3. Kennedy notes that in the wars between Britain and France before 1815, the key to victory was building a coalition of countries so that "a belligerent whose resources were fading could keep itself in the fight."[3]

4. A Yale historian claims that the Anglo-French wars lasted longer when the opponents were able to form economic coalitions with other states: "a belligerent whose resources were fading would look to a more powerful ally for loans and reinforcements in order to keep itself in the fight."[4]

5. The Anglo-French wars between 1689 and 1815 were, as Kennedy has pointed out, "such expensive and exhausting conflicts . . . [that] each side desperately required . . . 'money, money, and yet more money.'"[5]

Chicago (CMS) documentation: identifying elements of sources

For help with this exercise, see the *Chicago* (CMS) identifying elements of sources section in your handbook.

Circle the letter of the correct answer for each question using information in the source provided.

SOURCE: AN ARTICLE IN A PERIODICAL

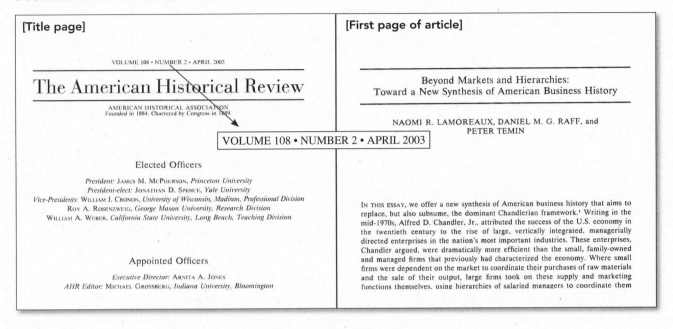

1. How would you begin a *Chicago*-style bibliography entry for this source?

    a. Lamoreaux, Naomi R., Daniel M. G. Raff, and Peter Temin. "Beyond Markets and Hierarchies: Toward a New Synthesis of American Business History."

    b. Lamoreaux, Naomi R., et al. "Beyond Markets and Hierarchies: Toward a New Synthesis of American Business History."

2. How would you cite the publication information for this article in a *Chicago*-style bibliography entry? The article begins on page 404 and ends on page 433.

    a. *American Historical Review* 108, no. 2 (2003): 404-33.

    b. *American Historical Review* 108.2 (2003): 404-33.

[Title page]

Black Athena

The Afroasiatic Roots
of Classical Civilization

VOLUME I
The Fabrication of Ancient Greece 1785–1985

Martin Bernal

Rutgers University Press
New Brunswick, New Jersey

[Copyright page]

First published in the United States by
Rutgers University Press, 1987
Fifth cloth and eighth paperback printing, April 1994
First published in Great Britain by
Free Association Books, 1987

© Martin Bernal 1987

Library of Congress Cataloging-in-Publication Data

Bernal, Martin
  Black Athena.
  (The fabrication of ancient Greece, 1785–1985; v. 1)
  Bibliography: p.
  Includes index.
  1. Greece—Civilization—Egyptian influences.
  2. Greece—Civilization—Phoenician influences.
  3. Greece—Civilization—To 146 B.C.   I. Title.
  II. Title: Afroasiatic roots of classical civilization.
  III. Series: Bernal, Martin. Fabrication of ancient
  Greece, 1785–1985; v. 1.
  DF78.B398   1987   949.5   87–16408
  ISBN 0-8135-1276-X
  ISBN 0-8135-1277-8 (pbk.)

Manufactured in the United States of America
All rights reserved

The publication of *Black Athena* was aided by
the Hull Memorial Publication Fund
of Cornell University.

---

3. How would you prepare a *Chicago*-style bibliography entry for this source?

a. Bernal, Martin. *Black Athena: The Afroasiatic Roots of Classical Civilization.* Vol. 1. New Brunswick, NJ: Rutgers University Press, 1987.

b. Bernal, Martin. *The Fabrication of Ancient Greece 1785-1985.* Vol. 1 of *Black Athena: The Afroasiatic Roots of Classical Civilization.* New Brunswick, NJ: Rutgers University Press, 1987.

Hacker/Sommers, *Working with Sources: Exercises for
Hacker Handbooks* (Boston: Bedford, 2018)

SOURCE: AN ARTICLE FROM A DATABASE

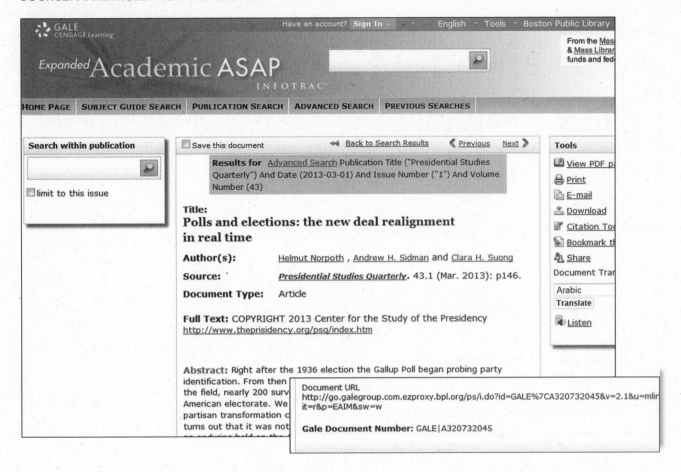

4. How would you cite the publication information for the periodical in this database record?

    a. *Presidential Studies Quarterly* 43, no. 1 (2013): 146+.

    b. *Presidential Studies Quarterly* 43 (March 2013): 146+.

5. What information would you place at the end of the entry, after the page number?

    a. Expanded Academic ASAP

    b. http://www.thepresidency.org

[Title page]

FLORENTINE HISTORIES

by

NICCOLÒ MACHIAVELLI

A New Translation by

LAURA F. BANFIELD

and

HARVEY C. MANSFIELD, JR.

With an Introduction by Harvey C. Mansfield, Jr.

PRINCETON UNIVERSITY PRESS
PRINCETON, NEW JERSEY

Republished with permission of Princeton University Press, from Florentine Histories by Niccolò Machiavelli. Translated by Laura F. Banfield & Harvey C. Mansfield Jr. 1990; permission conveyed through Copyright Clearance Center, Inc.

6. How would you begin a *Chicago*-style bibliography entry for this source?

   a. Banfield, Laura F., and Harvey C. Mansfield Jr., trans. *Florentine Histories.*

   b. Machiavelli, Niccolò. *Florentine Histories.* Translated by Laura F. Banfield and Harvey C. Mansfield Jr.

Hacker/Sommers, *Working with Sources: Exercises for Hacker Handbooks* (Boston: Bedford, 2018)

7. How would you begin a *Chicago*-style bibliography entry for this source?

   a. Scammell, Michael. "The Russian Nobility under the Red Terror." Review of *Former People: The Final Days of the Russian Aristocracy*, by Douglas Smith.

   b. Smith, Douglas. *Former People: The Final Days of the Russian Aristocracy*.

8. How would you cite the publication information for this source in a *Chicago*-style bibliography entry? (Page references are not included because the source is not paginated online.)

   a. *New York Review of Books,* March 7, 2013. http://www.nybooks.com/articles/archives/2013/mar/07/russian-nobility-under-red-terror.

   b. *New York Review of Books,* 7 Mar. 2013. http://www.nybooks.com/articles/archives/2013/mar/07/russian-nobility-under-red-terror.

SOURCE: A SHORT DOCUMENT FROM A WEBSITE

[Home page]

[Internal page]

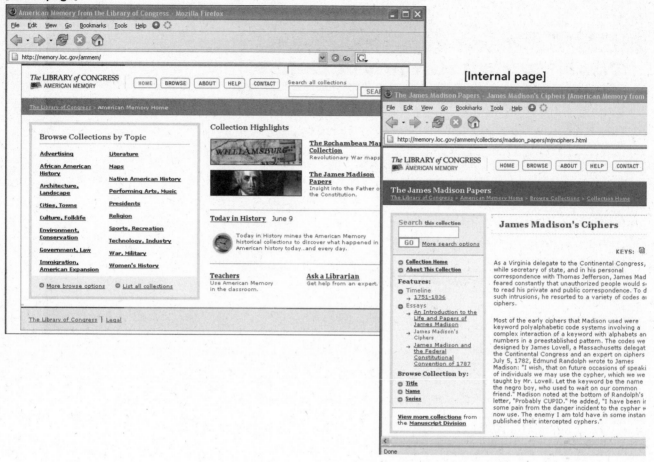

9. What would you cite as the sponsor of this source in a *Chicago*-style bibliography entry?

   a. Library of Congress

   b. No sponsor given

10. What is the correct *Chicago*-style bibliography entry for this source? (The site does not give an update date; the student accessed the site on April 3, 2013.)

   a. Library of Congress. "James Madison's Ciphers." American Memory. Accessed April 3, 2013. http://memory.loc.gov/ammem/collections/madison_papers/mjmciphers.html.

   b. "James Madison's Ciphers." American Memory. Library of Congress. Accessed April 3, 2013. http://memory.loc.gov/ammem/collections/madison_papers/mjmciphers.html.

Hacker/Sommers, *Working with Sources: Exercises for Hacker Handbooks* (Boston: Bedford, 2018)

Chicago (CMS) documentation: notes 1

For help with this exercise, see the *Chicago* (CMS) notes section in your handbook.

Circle the letter of the *Chicago* note that is handled correctly.

EXAMPLE
The student has quoted from page 141 of *Cities Then and Now*, by Jim Antoniou; the book was published in New York in 1994 by Macmillan. This is the first reference to the book in the paper.

a.　　　1. Jim Antoniou, *Cities Then and Now* (New York: Macmillan, 1994), p. 141.

(b.)　　1. Jim Antoniou, *Cities Then and Now* (New York: Macmillan, 1994), 141.

1. The student has quoted from page 48 of the third edition of *The AIA Guide to New York City*, by Elliot Willensky and Norval White; the book was published in 1988 in San Diego by Harcourt Brace Jovanovich. This is the first reference to the source in this paper.

    a.　　　1. Elliot Willensky and Norval White, *The AIA Guide to New York City*, 3rd ed. (San Diego: Harcourt Brace Jovanovich, 1988), 48.

    b.　　　1. Willensky, Elliot, and Norval White, *The AIA Guide to New York City*, 3rd ed. (San Diego: Harcourt Brace Jovanovich, 1988), 48.

2. The student has quoted from page 140 of *Cities Then and Now*, by Jim Antoniou; the book was published in New York in 1994 by Macmillan. This is the second reference to this source in the paper, and it does not immediately follow the first reference.

    a.　　　2. Jim Antoniou, *Cities Then and Now* (New York: Macmillan, 1994), 140.

    b.　　　2. Antoniou, *Cities Then and Now*, 140.

3. The student has summarized information found on pages 16-17 of *Low Life*, by Luc Santé, a book published in New York by Farrar, Straus and Giroux in 1991. This is the second reference to the book in the paper, and it immediately follows the first reference.

    a.　　　3. Santé, 16-17.

    b.　　　3. Santé, *Low Life*, 16-17.

4. The student has quoted from page 7 of an article in the *Bridge*, volume 32, issue 1, published in 2002. The article, by Leslie E. Robertson, is titled "Reflections on the World Trade Center." This is the first reference to the article in the paper.

    a.　　　4. Leslie E. Robertson, "Reflections on the World Trade Center," *Bridge* 32, no. 1 (2002): 7.

    b.　　　4. Leslie E. Robertson. "Reflections on the World Trade Center." *Bridge* 32, no. 1 (2002): 7.

5. The student has quoted from page 76 of "Building Plans," by Paul Goldberger. The article appeared in the weekly magazine the *New Yorker* on September 24, 2001. This is the first reference to the article in the paper.

    a.   5. Paul Goldberger, "Building Plans," *New Yorker,* September 2001, 76.

    b.   5. Paul Goldberger, "Building Plans," *New Yorker,* September 24, 2001, 76.

6. The student has quoted from page 78 of "Building Plans," by Paul Goldberger. The article appeared in the *New Yorker* on September 24, 2001. This is the second reference to the article in the paper, and it does not immediately follow the first reference.

    a.   6. Paul Goldberger ("Building Plans") 78.

    b.   6. Goldberger, "Building Plans," 78.

7. The student has quoted from page 14 of *Far-Right Politics in Europe,* written by Jean-Yves Camus and Nicolas Lebourg, translated by Jane Marie Todd, and published in Cambridge by Harvard University Press in 2017. This is the second reference to the book in the paper, and it does not immediately follow the first reference.

    a.   7. Camus and Lebourg, *Far-Right Politics in Europe,* 14.

    b.   7. Camus and others, *Far-Right Politics in Europe,* 14.

8. The student has quoted from an interview with Brian Clark conducted by Matt Barrett. The interview, which appeared in an episode titled "Why the Towers Fell" on the television program *Nova,* was broadcast on April 30, 2002, on the Public Broadcasting System. The source is a broadcast interview, so there is no page number.

    a.   8. Matt Barrett, "Why the Towers Fell," *Nova,* PBS, April 2002.

    b.   8. Brian Clark, interview by Matt Barrett, "Why the Towers Fell," *Nova,* PBS, April 30, 2002.

9. The student has quoted from an article, "Wider Inquiry into Towers Is Proposed," by James Glanz. It appeared on May 2, 2002, in the online version of the *New York Times.* The URL is http://nytimes.com/2002/05/02/nyregion/02TOWE.html, and this is the first reference to the article in the paper.

    a.   9. James Glanz, "Wider Inquiry into Towers Is Proposed," *New York Times,* May 2, 2002, http://nytimes.com/2002/05/02/nyregion/02TOWE.html.

    b.   9. James Glanz, "Wider Inquiry into Towers Is Proposed," *New York Times,* May 2, 2002.

Hacker/Sommers, *Working with Sources: Exercises for Hacker Handbooks* (Boston: Bedford, 2018)

10. The student has summarized information from the article "Why Did the World Trade Center Collapse?" by Thomas W. Eagar and Christopher Musso. The article appeared in the online journal *JOM: The Journal of the Minerals, Metals, and Materials Society,* volume 53, issue 12, published in 2001. The URL of the article is http://www.tms.org/pubs/journals/JOM/0112/Eagar/Eagar-0112.html. This is the first reference to the article in the paper.

a. 10. Thomas W. Eagar and Christopher Musso, "Why Did the World Trade Center Collapse?" *JOM: The Journal of the Minerals, Metals, and Materials Society,* http://www.tms.org/pubs/journals/JOM/0112/Eagar/Eagar-0112.html.

b. 10. Thomas W. Eagar and Christopher Musso, "Why Did the World Trade Center Collapse?" *JOM: The Journal of the Minerals, Metals, and Materials Society* 53, no. 12 (2001), http://www.tms.org/pubs/journals/JOM/0112/Eagar/Eagar-0112.html.

Chicago (CMS) documentation: notes 2

For help with this exercise, see the *Chicago* (CMS) notes section in your handbook.

Circle the letter of the *Chicago* note that is handled correctly.

EXAMPLE

The writer is quoting from page 92 of *Chronicles of the Vikings: Records, Memorials, and Myths*, by R. I. Page; the book was published in Toronto in 1995 by University of Toronto Press. This is the first reference to the book in the paper.

a.　　　1. R. I. Page, *Chronicles of the Vikings: Records, Memorials, and Myths* (Toronto: University of Toronto Press, 1995), p. 92.

(b.)　　　1. R. I. Page, *Chronicles of the Vikings: Records, Memorials, and Myths* (Toronto: University of Toronto Press, 1995), 92.

1.　The student has quoted from page 7 of *Viking Age Iceland*, by Jesse L. Byock; the book was published in London in 2001 by Penguin Books. This is the first reference to the book in the paper.

a.　　　1. Byock, Jesse L., *Viking Age Iceland* (London: Penguin Books, 2001), 7.

b.　　　1. Jesse L. Byock, *Viking Age Iceland* (London: Penguin Books, 2001), 7.

2.　The student has quoted from page 92 of the book *Chronicles of the Vikings: Records, Memorials, and Myths*, by R. I. Page; the book was published in Toronto in 1995 by University of Toronto Press. This is the second reference to the book in the paper.

a.　　　2. Page, *Chronicles of the Vikings*, 92.

b.　　　2. R. I. Page, *Chronicles of the Vikings: Records, Memorials, and Myths* (Toronto: University of Toronto Press, 1995), 92.

3.　The writer has cited material from pages 271-72 of *An Introduction to Medieval Europe, 300-1500*, by James Westfall Thompson and Edgar Nathaniel Johnson; the book was published in New York by Norton in 1937. This is the second reference to the book in the paper.

a.　　　3. Thompson and Johnson, *Introduction to Medieval Europe*, 271-72.

b.　　　3. Thompson, *Introduction to Medieval Europe*, 271-72.

4.　The writer has summarized information found on page 132 of *Medieval Technology and Social Change*, by Lynn White Jr.; the book was published in London by Oxford University Press in 1962. This is the first reference to the book in the paper.

a.　　　4. Lynn White Jr., *Medieval Technology and Social Change* (London: Oxford University Press, 1962), 132.

b.　　　4. Lynn White Jr. *Medieval Technology and Social Change* (London: Oxford University Press, 1962). 132.

5. The student has quoted from page 55 of the anonymous "Graenlendinga Saga." The work is found in *The Vinland Sagas: The Norse Discovery of America,* which was translated by Magnus Magnusson and Hermann Pálsson. Penguin Books published the book in London in 1965. This is the first reference to the book in the paper.

a. 5. Anonymous, "Graenlendinga Saga," in *The Vinland Sagas: The Norse Discovery of America,* trans. Magnus Magnusson and Hermann Pálsson (London: Penguin Books, 1965), 55.

b. 5. "Graenlendinga Saga," in *The Vinland Sagas: The Norse Discovery of America,* trans. Magnus Magnusson and Hermann Pálsson (London: Penguin Books, 1965), 55.

6. The student has quoted from "A Saga of Discovery," a short document found on the website Vikings Discovery and Landing at L'anse aux Meadows. There is no author, and the site is sponsored by Library and Archives Canada. The URL for the document is http://collections .ic.gc.ca/vikings/rediscovery1.htm, and this is the first reference to the document in the paper. The article does not have an update date; the student accessed it on September 23, 2002.

a. 6. "A Saga of Discovery," Library and Archives Canada, accessed September 23, 2002, http:// collections.ic.gc.ca/vikings/rediscovery1.htm.

b. 6. "A Saga of Discovery," Vikings Discovery and Landing at L'anse aux Meadows, Library and Archives Canada, accessed September 23, 2002, http://collections.ic.gc.ca/vikings/rediscovery1 .htm.

7. The writer has quoted from page 109 of "Questions of Origin: Vikings, Vinland, and the Veracity of a Map," an article by Jessica Gorman in volume 162, issue 7, of the magazine *Science News,* published on August 17, 2002. This is the first reference to the article in the paper.

a. 7. Jessica Gorman, "Questions of Origin: Vikings, Vinland, and the Veracity of a Map," *Science News,* August 17, 2002, 109.

b. 7. Jessica Gorman, "Questions of Origin: Vikings, Vinland, and the Veracity of a Map," *Science News* 162, no. 7 (2002): 109.

8. The writer has quoted from page C1 of an article by John Noble Wilford, "Disputed Medieval Map Called Genuine After All." The article appeared in the *New York Times* on February 13, 1996. This is the first reference to the article in the paper.

a. 8. John Noble Wilford, "Disputed Medieval Map Called Genuine After All," *New York Times,* February 13, 1996, C1.

b. 8. John Noble Wilford, "Disputed Medieval Map Called Genuine After All," *New York Times,* February 13, 1996, sec. C.

Hacker/Sommers, *Working with Sources: Exercises for Hacker Handbooks* (Boston: Bedford, 2018)

9. The writer has quoted from John Noble Wilford's article "Disputed Medieval Map Called Genuine After All," which appeared on page C1 of the *New York Times* on February 13, 1996. This is the second reference to page C1 in the paper, and it immediately follows the first reference.

    a.   9. Wilford, "Disputed Medieval Map," sec. C.

    b.   9. "Disputed Medieval Map," sec. C.

10. The writer has quoted from a report by David Kestenbaum from August 5, 2002, titled "Is the Vinland Map a Fake?" The report is on the National Public Radio website, NPR, at http://www.npr.org/programs/morning/features/2002/aug/vinlandmap/index.html. This is the first reference to the source in the paper.

    a.   10. David Kestenbaum, "Is the Vinland Map a Fake?," NPR, August 5, 2002, http://www.npr .org/programs/morning/features/2002/aug/vinlandmap/index.html.

    b.   10. David Kestenbaum, "Is the Vinland Map a Fake?," NPR, National Public Radio, August 5, 2002, http://www.npr.org/programs/morning/features/2002/aug/vinlandmap/index.html.

Chicago (CMS) documentation: notes 3

For help with this exercise, see the *Chicago* (CMS) notes section in your handbook.

Circle the letter of the *Chicago* note that is handled correctly.

EXAMPLE

The student has quoted from page 111 of a book by Bill Gertz, *Breakdown: How America's Intelligence Failures Led to September 11*, published in Washington, DC, in 2002 by Regnery Publishing.

(a.)   1. Bill Gertz, *Breakdown: How America's Intelligence Failures Led to September 11* (Washington, DC: Regnery, 2002), 111.

b.   1. Gertz, Bill. *Breakdown: How America's Intelligence Failures Led to September 11.* Washington, DC: Regnery, 2002, 111.

1. The student has quoted from page 33 of a book by Victor Marchetti and John D. Marks, *The CIA and the Cult of Intelligence*, published in New York in 1974 by Dell Publishing Company. This is the first reference to the source in the paper.

    a.   1. Marchetti, Victor, and John D. Marks, *The CIA and the Cult of Intelligence* (New York: Dell, 1974), 33.

    b.   1. Victor Marchetti and John D. Marks, *The CIA and the Cult of Intelligence* (New York: Dell, 1974), 33.

2. The student has quoted from page 77 of an article, "The Stovepipe," by Seymour M. Hersh. It appeared in the *New Yorker* magazine on October 27, 2003. This is the first reference to the source in the paper.

    a.   2. Seymour M. Hersh, "The Stovepipe," *New Yorker*, Oct. 27, 2003, 77.

    b.   2. Seymour M. Hersh, "The Stovepipe," *New Yorker*, October 27, 2003, 77.

3. The student has paraphrased a passage from page A12 of a *New York Times* article, "Tenet Concedes Gaps in CIA Data on Iraq Weapons," by Douglas Jehl, which appeared on February 6, 2004. The article began on page A1 and continued on page A12. This is the first reference to the source in the paper.

    a.   3. Douglas Jehl, "Tenet Concedes Gaps in CIA Data on Iraq Weapons," *New York Times*, 6 February 2004, sec. A.

    b.   3. Douglas Jehl, "Tenet Concedes Gaps in CIA Data on Iraq Weapons," *New York Times*, February 6, 2004, sec. A.

4. The student has quoted from page 370 of an essay, "The Trouble with the CIA," by Thomas Powers, published in 2002 in the book *Intelligence Wars: American Secret History from Hitler to Al-Qaeda*. The book, a collection of Powers's essays, was published in New York by New York Review Books in 2002. This is the first reference to the source in the paper.

a. 4. Thomas Powers, "The Trouble with the CIA," in *Intelligence Wars: American Secret History from Hitler to Al-Qaeda* (New York: New York Review Books, 2002), 370.

b. 4. Thomas Powers, "The Trouble with the CIA," *Intelligence Wars: American Secret History from Hitler to Al-Qaeda* (New York: New York Review Books, 2002), 370.

5. The student has summarized an article, "CIA Intelligence Reports Seven Months before 9/11 Said Iraq Posed No Threat to US, Containment Was Working," by Jason Leopold. The article appeared on the website of the online magazine *Common Dreams* on February 17, 2004. The URL for the article is http://www.commondreams.org/views04/0217-12.htm. This is the first reference to the source in the paper.

a. 5. Jason Leopold, "CIA Intelligence Reports Seven Months before 9/11 Said Iraq Posed No Threat to US, Containment Was Working," *Common Dreams*, February 17, 2004, http://www .commondreams.org/views04/0217-12.htm.

b. 5. Jason Leopold, "CIA Intelligence Reports Seven Months before 9/11 Said Iraq Posed No Threat to US, Containment Was Working," *Common Dreams*, February 17, 2004, <http://www .commondreams.org/views04/0217-12.htm>.

6. The student has paraphrased material from the article "Why Can't Uncle Sam Spy?" by Anthony York. The article appeared in the online magazine *Salon* on September 18, 2001. The article's URL is http://archive.salon.com/news/feature/2001/09/18/spooks/index1.html. This is the first reference to the source in the paper.

a. 6. Anthony York, "Why Can't Uncle Sam Spy?," September 18, 2001, *Salon*, http://archive .salon.com/news/feature/2001/09/18/spooks/index1.html.

b. 6. Anthony York, "Why Can't Uncle Sam Spy?," *Salon*, September 18, 2001, http://archive .salon.com/news/feature/2001/09/18/spooks/index1.html.

7. The student has quoted from page 11 of an unsigned article, "Sincere Deceivers," published in the magazine *The Economist* on July 17, 2004. This is the first reference to the source in the paper.

a. 7. "Sincere Deceivers," *Economist*, July 17, 2004, 11.

b. 7. *Economist*, "Sincere Deceivers," July 17, 2004, 11.

Hacker/Sommers, *Working with Sources: Exercises for Hacker Handbooks* (Boston: Bedford, 2018)

8. The student has quoted from page 6 of a review of *The 9/11 Commission Report: Final Report of the National Commission on Terrorist Attacks upon the United States,* published by Norton in New York in 2004. The review, by Elizabeth Drew, was titled "Pinning the Blame" and was printed in the *New York Review of Books* on September 23, 2004. This is the first reference to the source in the paper.

   a.   8. Elizabeth Drew, "Pinning the Blame," review of *The 9/11 Commission Report: Final Report of the National Commission on Terrorist Attacks upon the United States, New York Review of Books,* September 23, 2004, 6.

   b.   8. Elizabeth Drew, "Pinning the Blame," review of *The 9/11 Commission Report: Final Report of the National Commission on Terrorist Attacks upon the United States* (New York: Norton, 2004), *New York Review of Books,* September 23, 2004, 6.

9. The student has quoted from page 14 of the article "In a Run-up to War, How Do We Report Intelligently on Intelligence?" written by Ted Gup in the March-April 2003 issue of *Columbia Journalism Review.* This is the second citation of the article in the paper. The first citation was in note 2.

   a.   9. Gup, 14.

   b.   9. Gup, "In a Run-up to War," 14.

10. The student has paraphrased a passage from page 81 of an article by Kenneth M. Pollack titled "Spies, Lies, and Weapons: What Went Wrong." The article appeared in the January-February 2004 issue of the *Atlantic.* This is the second citation of the article in the paper. The first citation was in note 9, citing page 80 of the article.

   a.   10. Pollack, "Spies, Lies, and Weapons," 81.

   b.   10. "Spies, Lies, and Weapons," 81.

Chicago (CMS) documentation: bibliography 1

For help with this exercise, see the section on *Chicago* (CMS) bibliography in your handbook.

Circle the letter of the *Chicago* bibliography entry that is handled correctly.

EXAMPLE

The student has quoted from a book, *Bad Land: An American Romance,* by Jonathan Raban. It was published in New York in 1996 by Pantheon Books.

a. Jonathan Raban. *Bad Land.* New York: Pantheon Books, 1996.

b. Raban, Jonathan. *Bad Land: An American Romance.* New York: Pantheon Books, 1996.

1. The student has paraphrased material from a book, *The Age of Reform: From Bryan to F.D.R.,* by Richard Hofstadter. It was published in 1955 in New York by Vintage Books.

   a. Richard Hofstadter. *The Age of Reform: From Bryan to F.D.R.* New York: Vintage Books, 1955.

   b. Hofstadter, Richard. *The Age of Reform: From Bryan to F.D.R.* New York: Vintage Books, 1955.

2. The student has cited the fifth edition of a book, *The American Promise: A History of the United States,* by James L. Roark, Michael P. Johnson, Patricia Cline Cohen, Sarah Stage, and Susan M. Hartmann. The book was published in Boston by Bedford/St. Martin's in 2012.

   a. Roark, James L., Michael P. Johnson, Patricia Cline Cohen, Sarah Stage, and Susan M. Hartmann. *The American Promise: A History of the United States.* 5th ed. Boston: Bedford/St. Martin's, 2012.

   b. Roark, James L., et al. *The American Promise: A History of the United States.* 5th ed. Boston: Bedford/St. Martin's, 2012.

3. The student has summarized material from an article, "America and Its Discontents," by Lilian and Oscar Handlin. The article appears on pages 15-37 of volume 64, issue 1, of the journal *American Scholar,* published in 1995.

   a. Handlin, Lilian and Oscar. "America and Its Discontents." *American Scholar* 64, no. 1: 15-37.

   b. Handlin, Lilian and Oscar. "America and Its Discontents." *American Scholar* 64, no. 1 (1995): 15-37.

4. The student has quoted from the article "Dust, the Thermostat: How Tiny Airborne Particles Manipulate Global Climate," by Sid Perkins, which appears on pages 200-202 of the September 29, 2001, edition of the magazine *Science News* (volume 160, issue 13).

   a. Perkins, Sid. "Dust, the Thermostat: How Tiny Airborne Particles Manipulate Global Climate." *Science News,* September 29, 2001, 200-202.

   b. Perkins, Sid. "Dust, the Thermostat: How Tiny Airborne Particles Manipulate Global Climate." *Science News,* September 29, 2001, 160 (13): 200-202.

5. The student has paraphrased material from an essay, "Learning from the Prairie," by Scott Russell Sanders. It appears on pages 3-15 of the anthology *The New Agrarianism: Land, Culture, and the Community of Life,* edited by Eric T. Freyfogle. The book was published in Washington, DC, in 2001 by Island Press.

   a. Sanders, Scott Russell. "Learning from the Prairie." In *The New Agrarianism: Land, Culture, and the Community of Life,* edited by Eric T. Freyfogle, 3-15. Washington, DC: Island Press, 2001.

   b. Sanders, Scott Russell. "Learning from the Prairie." In *The New Agrarianism: Land, Culture, and the Community of Life.* Ed. Eric T. Freyfogle, 3-15. Washington, DC: Island Press, 2001.

6. The student has cited an unpublished PhD dissertation, "The Righteous Cause: Some Religious Aspects of Kansas Populism," by Leland Levi Lengel. The dissertation was accepted in Eugene, Oregon, by the University of Oregon in 1968 and is listed in the ProQuest database.

   a. Lengel, Leland Levi. "The Righteous Cause: Some Religious Aspects of Kansas Populism." Unpublished PhD diss., University of Oregon, 1968. ProQuest.

   b. Lengel, Leland Levi. "The Righteous Cause: Some Religious Aspects of Kansas Populism." PhD diss., University of Oregon, 1968. ProQuest.

7. The student has quoted from an article, "Biography of Hugh Hammond Bennett," appearing on the website of the National Resources Conservation Service, a division of the US Department of Agriculture (the site's sponsor). The title of the site is National Resources Conservation Service. No author is listed for the article, and no date of posting is given. The date of access was February 29, 2004. The URL of the article is http://www.nrcs.usda.gov/about/history/bennett.html.

   a. "Biography of Hugh Hammond Bennett." National Resources Conservation Service. Accessed February 29, 2004. http://www.nrcs.usda.gov/about/history/bennett.html.

   b. "Biography of Hugh Hammond Bennett." National Resources Conservation Service. US Department of Agriculture. Accessed February 29, 2004. http://www.nrcs.usda.gov/about/history/bennett.html.

8. The student has cited a journal article accessed through a database. The article is "Small Farms, Externalities, and the Dust Bowl of the 1930s," by Zeynep K. Hansen and Gary D. Libecap. It appeared on pages 665-95 in the *Journal of Political Economy,* dated June 2004, volume 112, issue 3. The database is JSTOR, and the article is assigned the persistent URL http://www.jstor.org/stable/3555186.

   a. Hansen, Zeynep K., and Gary D. Libecap. "Small Farms, Externalities, and the Dust Bowl of the 1930s." *Journal of Political Economy* 112, no. 3 (2004): 665-95. http://www.jstor.org/stable/3555186.

   b. Hansen, Zeynep K., and Gary D. Libecap. "Small Farms, Externalities, and the Dust Bowl of the 1930s." *Journal of Political Economy* 112, no. 3 (2004): 665-95. JSTOR.

Hacker/Sommers, *Working with Sources: Exercises for Hacker Handbooks* (Boston: Bedford, 2018)

9. The student has cited an article, "Another One Bites the Dust," by Lester R. Brown, which appeared in an online publication, *Grist Magazine*, on May 29, 2001. The URL of the article is http://www.gristmagazine.com/maindish/brown052901.asp.

   a. Brown, Lester R. "Another One Bites the Dust." http://www.gristmagazine.com/maindish/brown052901.asp.

   b. Brown, Lester R. "Another One Bites the Dust." *Grist Magazine,* May 29, 2001. http://www.gristmagazine.com/maindish/brown052901.asp.

10. The student has quoted dialogue from the film *The Grapes of Wrath*, directed by John Ford. The film was produced in 1940 by Twentieth Century Fox. The student viewed a DVD released in 2004 by Fox Home Entertainment in Beverly Hills, California.

    a. Ford, John, dir. *The Grapes of Wrath.* 1940; Beverly Hills, CA: Fox Home Entertainment, 2004. DVD.

    b. *The Grapes of Wrath.* Directed by John Ford. 1940; Beverly Hills, CA: Fox Home Entertainment, 2004. DVD.

Chicago (CMS) documentation: bibliography 2

For help with this exercise, see the section on *Chicago* (CMS) bibliography in your handbook.

Circle the letter of the *Chicago* bibliography entry that is handled correctly.

EXAMPLE

The student has summarized information from a book titled *Pearl Harbor: Warning and Decision*, written by Roberta Wohlstetter and published in 1962 by Stanford University Press in Stanford, California.

a. Wohlstetter, Roberta. *Pearl Harbor: Warning and Decision* (Stanford: Stanford University Press, 1962).

b. Wohlstetter, Roberta. *Pearl Harbor: Warning and Decision.* Stanford: Stanford University Press, 1962.

1. The student has quoted from an article appearing on page A36 of the December 7, 2008, *New York Times* titled "Report Debunks Theory That the US Heard a Coded Warning about Pearl Harbor," by Sam Roberts.

   a. Roberts, Sam. "Report Debunks Theory That the US Heard a Coded Warning about Pearl Harbor." *New York Times*, December 7, 2008, A36.

   b. Roberts, Sam. "Report Debunks Theory That the US Heard a Coded Warning about Pearl Harbor." *New York Times*, December 7, 2008, sec. A.

2. The student has summarized material from an essay, "Pearl Harbor as an Intelligence Failure," written by David Kahn and printed on pages 158-96 of the book *Pearl Harbor and the Coming of the Pacific War: A Brief History with Documents and Essays*, edited by Akira Iriye. The book was published in Boston in 1999 by Bedford/St. Martin's and is part of a series called the Bedford Series in History and Culture.

   a. Kahn, David. "Pearl Harbor as an Intelligence Failure." In *Pearl Harbor and the Coming of the Pacific War: A Brief History with Documents and Essays*, edited by Akira Iriye, 158-96. Bedford Series in History and Culture. Boston: Bedford/St. Martin's, 1999.

   b. Iriye, Akira, ed. *Pearl Harbor and the Coming of the Pacific War: A Brief History with Documents and Essays.* "Pearl Harbor as an Intelligence Failure," by David Kahn, 158-96. Bedford Series in History and Culture. Boston: Bedford/St. Martin's, 1999.

3. The student has quoted material from an untitled review of the book *A Date Which Will Live: Pearl Harbor in American Memory*, by Emily S. Rosenberg. The book was published in 2003 in Durham, NC, by Duke University Press. The review was written by Naoko Shibusawa and appears on page 1519 of the *Journal of American History*, volume 91, issue 4, published in 2005.

   a. Rosenberg, Emily S. *A Date Which Will Live: Pearl Harbor in American Memory.* Reviewed by Naoko Shibusawa. *Journal of American History* 91, no. 4 (2005): 1519.

   b. Shibusawa, Naoko. Review of *A Date Which Will Live: Pearl Harbor in American Memory*, by Emily S. Rosenberg. *Journal of American History* 91, no. 4 (2005): 1519.

4. The student has summarized information from an article appearing on pages 75-101 of the *Journal of Military History*, volume 58, issue 1, which was published in January 1994. The article is titled "Pinpointing Devastation: American Air Campaign Planning before Pearl Harbor" and was written by Mark Clodfelter.

   a. Clodfelter, Mark. "Pinpointing Devastation: American Air Campaign Planning before Pearl Harbor." *Journal of Military History* 58, no. 1: 75-101.

   b. Clodfelter, Mark. "Pinpointing Devastation: American Air Campaign Planning before Pearl Harbor." *Journal of Military History* 58, no. 1 (1994): 75-101.

5. The student has quoted material from a letter published on pages 184-87 of the book *War Letters: Extraordinary Correspondence from American Wars*, which was edited by Andrew Carroll. The letter was written by Paul E. Spangler on December 17, 1941, and was sent to Izee Reds. The book was published in New York by Scribner in 2001.

   a. Spangler, Paul E. Paul E. Spangler to Izee Reds, 17 December 1941. In *War Letters: Extraordinary Correspondence from American Wars*, edited by Andrew Carroll, 184-87. New York: Scribner, 2001.

   b. Spangler, Paul E. Paul E. Spangler to Izee Reds, December 17, 1941. In *War Letters: Extraordinary Correspondence from American Wars*, edited by Andrew Carroll, 184-87. New York: Scribner, 2001.

6. The student has paraphrased material from the short work "United States Naval Base, Pearl Harbor," on the website Aviation: From Sand Dunes to Sonic Booms. There is no named author and no update date. The site is sponsored by the National Park Service. The student accessed the material at http://www.nps.gov/nr/travel/aviation/prl.htm on December 3, 2008.

   a. "United States Naval Base, Pearl Harbor." Aviation: From Sand Dunes to Sonic Booms. National Park Service. Accessed December 3, 2008. http://www.nps.gov/nr/travel/aviation/prl.htm.

   b. "United States Naval Base, Pearl Harbor." Aviation: From Sand Dunes to Sonic Booms. National Park Service. http://www.nps.gov/nr/travel/aviation/prl.htm.

7. The student has paraphrased material from a posting to the H-war discussion list written by Christopher Koontz on January 22, 2009. The title of the posting is "Trivialization of History," and the URL is http://www.h-net.org/logsearch/?phrase=pearl+harbor&type=keyword&hitlimit=25&field=&nojg=on&smonth=00&syear=1989&emonth=11&eyear=2029&order=-@DPB.

   a. Koontz, Christopher. "Trivialization of History." Posting to the H-war discussion list. January 22, 2009. http://www.h-net.org/logsearch/?phrase=pearl+harbor&type=keyword&hitlimit=25&field=&nojg=on&smonth=00&syear=1989&emonth=11&eyear=2029&order=-@DPB.

   b. No entry; discussion list postings are not included in a CMS bibliography.

Hacker/Sommers, *Working with Sources: Exercises for Hacker Handbooks* (Boston: Bedford, 2018)

8. The student has summarized a few paragraphs from pages 648-53 of the biography *Franklin Delano Roosevelt: Champion of Freedom*, by Conrad Black. The book was published in New York by PublicAffairs in 2003.

    a. Black, Conrad. *Franklin Delano Roosevelt: Champion of Freedom*, 648-53. New York: PublicAffairs, 2003.

    b. Black, Conrad. *Franklin Delano Roosevelt: Champion of Freedom*. New York: PublicAffairs, 2003.

9. The student has quoted dialogue from the documentary movie *Pearl Harbor: Legacy of Attack*, which was directed by Michael Rosenfeld and Kurt Wolfinger and narrated by Tom Brokaw. The student viewed the 2006 DVD version; the original was released in 2001. The producer/distributor is National Geographic Video in Washington, DC.

    a. Rosenfeld, Michael, and Kurt Wolfinger, dirs. *Pearl Harbor: Legacy of Attack*. 2001; Washington, DC: National Geographic Video, 2006. DVD.

    b. Rosenfeld, Michael, and Kurt Wolfinger, dirs. Narrated by Tom Brokaw. *Pearl Harbor: Legacy of Attack*. 2001; Washington, DC: National Geographic Video, DVD.

10. The student has quoted from an article titled "Unlocking a Photograph's Secrets (Pearl Harbor Attack, 1941)." The article has no named author and appeared in *American History*, volume 30, issue 1, in April 1995 on page 74. The student found the article in the Expanded Academic ASAP database. The database does not give a DOI (digital object identifier).

    a. "Unlocking a Photograph's Secrets (Pearl Harbor Attack, 1941)." *American History* 30, no. 1 (1995): 74. Expanded Academic ASAP.

    b. "Unlocking a Photograph's Secrets (Pearl Harbor Attack, 1941)." *American History* 30, no. 1 (1995): 74.

Chicago (CMS) documentation: bibliography 3

For help with this exercise, see the section on *Chicago* (CMS) bibliography in your handbook.

Circle the letter of the *Chicago* bibliography entry that is handled correctly.

EXAMPLE

The student has summarized information from the book *A History of Modern Russia: From Nicholas II to Vladimir Putin*, by Robert Service. The book was published in 2005 by Harvard University Press in Cambridge, MA.

a. Robert Service. *A History of Modern Russia: From Nicholas II to Vladimir Putin*. Cambridge, MA: Harvard University Press, 2005.

b. Service, Robert. *A History of Modern Russia: From Nicholas II to Vladimir Putin*. Cambridge, MA: Harvard University Press, 2005.

1. The student has quoted material from the book *The Communist Manifesto*, by Karl Marx and Friedrich Engels. The book was originally published in 1888 and was released online by Project Gutenberg in 2005. The student accessed the book at http://www.gutenberg.org /etext/61. The original publisher is unknown.

   a. Marx, Karl, and Friedrich Engels. *The Communist Manifesto*. 1888. Project Gutenberg, 2005. http:// www.gutenberg.org/etext/61.

   b. Marx, Karl, and Engels, Friedrich. *The Communist Manifesto*. 1888. Project Gutenberg, 2005. http:// www.gutenberg.org/etext/61.

2. The student has summarized material from the article "Soviet and American Communist Parties" on the website Soviet Archives Exhibit. The article and the website do not have an author. The site is sponsored by the Library of Congress. The URL for the article is http://www.ibiblio.org/expo/soviet .exhibit/party.html, and the student accessed the site on January 13, 2009.

   a. Anonymous. "Soviet and American Communist Parties." Soviet Archives Exhibit. Library of Congress. Accessed January 13, 2009. http://www.ibiblio.org/expo/soviet.exhibit/party .html.

   b. "Soviet and American Communist Parties." Soviet Archives Exhibit. Library of Congress. Accessed January 13, 2009. http://www.ibiblio.org/expo/soviet.exhibit/party.html.

3. Near the beginning of the research paper, the student has summarized material from the book *Why Did the Soviet Union Collapse? Understanding Historical Change*, by Robert W. Strayer. The book was published

by M. E. Sharpe in 1998 in Armonk, NY. Near the end of the paper, the student has summarized material from an article by Robert W. Strayer titled "Decolonization, Democratization, and Communist Reform: The Soviet Collapse in Comparative Perspective." The article appeared on pages 375-406 of *Journal of World History*, volume 12, issue 2, in 2001.

a. Strayer, Robert W. "Decolonization, Democratization, and Communist Reform: The Soviet Collapse in Comparative Perspective." *Journal of World History* 12, no. 2 (2001): 375-406.

------. *Why Did the Soviet Union Collapse? Understanding Historical Change.* Armonk, NY: M. E. Sharpe, 1998.

b. Strayer, Robert W. *Why Did the Soviet Union Collapse? Understanding Historical Change.* Armonk, NY: M. E. Sharpe, 1998.

------. "Decolonization, Democratization, and Communist Reform: The Soviet Collapse in Comparative Perspective." *Journal of World History* 12, no. 2 (2001): 375-406.

4. The student has quoted from an email message received from a relative, Max Pavlovsky, who lived in the Soviet Union during his childhood. The email was sent to the student on December 28, 2008.

a. Pavlovsky, Max. Email message to the author. December 28, 2008.

b. No entry in the bibliography for email messages

5. The student has quoted from the film *Battleship Potemkin*, directed by Sergei Eisenstein in 1925. The student viewed a DVD that was distributed in 2004 by Delta Entertainment in Los Angeles.

a. *Battleship Potemkin*. Directed by Sergei Eisenstein. Los Angeles: Delta Entertainment, 2004. DVD.

b. Eisenstein, Sergei, dir. *Battleship Potemkin*. 1925; Los Angeles: Delta Entertainment, 2004. DVD.

6. The student has quoted material from page 202 of the book *The Rise of Russia and the Fall of the Soviet Empire*, by John B. Dunlop. The book was published in 1993 by Princeton University Press. The material being quoted originally appeared on page 64 in a September 2, 1991, *Newsweek* article by Henry A. Kissinger titled "Dealing with a New Russia."

a. Kissinger, Henry A. "Dealing with a New Russia." *Newsweek*, September 2, 1991, 64. Quoted in John B. Dunlop, *The Rise of Russia and the Fall of the Soviet Empire* (Princeton, NJ: Princeton University Press, 1993), 202.

b. Kissinger, Henry A. "Dealing with a New Russia." Quoted in John B. Dunlop, *The Rise of Russia and the Fall of the Soviet Empire* (Princeton, NJ: Princeton University Press, 1993), 202.

Hacker/Sommers, *Working with Sources: Exercises for Hacker Handbooks* (Boston: Bedford, 2018)

7. The student has paraphrased material from the article "Redesigning History in Contemporary Russia," by Catherine Merridale. The article appeared on pages 13-28 of the *Journal of Contemporary History*, volume 38, issue 1, which was published in 2003. The student accessed the article on February 16, 2009, from the JSTOR database, which assigns the article the stable URL http://www.jstor.org/stable/3180694.

   a. Merridale, Catherine. "Redesigning History in Contemporary Russia." *Journal of Contemporary History* 38, no. 1 (2003): 13-28. http://www.jstor.org/stable/3180694.

   b. Merridale, Catherine. "Redesigning History in Contemporary Russia." *Journal of Contemporary History*. http://www.jstor.org/stable/3180694.

8. The student has summarized information from an article titled "Narrating the Russian Revolution: Institutionalism and Continuity across Regime Change," by Don K. Rowney. The article appeared on pages 79-105 of *Comparative Studies in Society and History*, volume 47, issue 1, published in 2005.

   a. Rowney, Don K. "Narrating the Russian Revolution: Institutionalism and Continuity across Regime Change." *Comparative Studies in Society and History* 47, no. 1 (2005): 79-105.

   b. Rowney, Don K. "Narrating the Russian Revolution: Institutionalism and Continuity across Regime Change." *Comparative Studies in Society and History* (2005): 79-105.

9. The student has paraphrased material from a newspaper article titled "Russians Get New, Fond Glimpse of the Last Czar," by Courtney Weaver. The article appeared on page 8 in section A of the July 20, 2008, *New York Times*.

   a. Weaver, Courtney. "Russians Get New, Fond Glimpse of the Last Czar." *New York Times*, July 20, 2008, sec. A, p. 8.

   b. Weaver, Courtney. "Russians Get New, Fond Glimpse of the Last Czar." *New York Times*, July 20, 2008, sec. A.

10. The student is quoting material from an article titled "Russia's Struggle with the Language of Marketing in the Communist and Post-Communist Eras," by Nigel Holden, Andrei Kuznetsov, and Jeryl Whitelock. The article appeared on pages 474-88 of *Business History*, volume 50, issue 4, published in 2008.

   a. Holden, Nigel, Andrei Kuznetsov, and Jeryl Whitelock. "Russia's Struggle with the Language of Marketing in the Communist and Post-Communist Eras." *Business History* 50, no. 4 (2008): 474-88.

   b. Holden, Nigel, et al. "Russia's Struggle with the Language of Marketing in the Communist and Post-Communist Eras." *Business History* 50, no. 4 (2008): 474-88.

Chicago (CMS) documentation

For help with this exercise, see the section on *Chicago* (CMS) documentation in your handbook.

Write "true" if the statement is true or "false" if it is false.

1. Each summary, paraphrase, and direct quotation from a source cited in the paper requires a footnote or an endnote.

2. The bibliography should include only works that are cited with notes in the text of the paper.

3. If a source has already been cited in the paper, no note is needed for further references to that source.

4. When a work is cited in two consecutive notes, the note for the second citation should include only the page number.

5. The bibliography is organized alphabetically by authors' (or editors') last names (or by title for a work with no author).

6. The note and bibliography entry for a source found on a website should include the URL in angle brackets.

7. A note should list the author's first name first; a bibliography entry should list the last name first.

8. Both the note and its corresponding bibliography entry should begin with a paragraph-style indent.

9. Notes may be given at the foot of a page or they may appear at the end of the paper, right before the bibliography.

10. Note numbers in the text of the paper appear in parentheses.

Hacker/Sommers, *Working with Sources: Exercises for Hacker Handbooks* (Boston: Bedford, 2018)

Answers to Exercises

Research questions, page 1

1. b. This question, which raises issues of debate, is intellectually challenging. The other question, which calls for a definition, is merely factual.
2. b. This question is focused enough (dealing with a specific region and a specific environmental problem) to cover adequately in ten to fifteen pages.
3. a. This question is intellectually challenging: To answer it, the writer will need to weigh evidence and judge the soundness of competing arguments. The other question leads simply to fact searching.
4. a. This question is focused on a specific demographic in a specific country and can be covered adequately in ten to fifteen pages.
5. b. This question is grounded in evidence; to answer it, the writer would need to rely on more than just speculation.
6. a. This question is challenging; it requires the writer to analyze and interpret historical evidence. The other question leads simply to fact searching.
7. b. This question, which raises issues of debate, is intellectually challenging. The other calls for factual evidence.
8. a. This question is intellectually challenging because it requires the writer to weigh evidence about a problem and its solution. The other question leads simply to fact searching.
9. b. A paper answering this question would be grounded in evidence and would require analysis of the effects on elementary education. The other question suggests that the writer will base the paper on moral beliefs.
10. b. This question is challenging because it leads to a causal analysis. The other question leads to a reporting of facts.

Thesis statements in MLA papers 1, page 3

1. b. This sentence makes an assertion that can be developed in a paper. The other version merely states facts.
2. b. This sentence makes a clear and focused assertion that can be argued in a paper. The other version is too vague.
3. a. This sentence makes an assertion that can lead to a historical analysis. The other version merely states a fact.
4. a. This thesis is limited to a narrow topic—laws that will aid the US government in fighting terrorist activities. The other version is too broad and too vague.
5. b. This sentence is focused and presents assertions that can be argued in a paper. The other is vague and does not make an assertion that can be argued in a paper.
6. b. This sentence makes a clear assertion and suggests an organizational plan for the paper. The other version merely gives a factual definition.
7. b. This thesis restricts the topic to one idea that the writer can develop with specific examples in a paper. The other version is too broad.
8. b. The other version merely states facts.
9. b. This thesis focuses on an idea that the writer can develop in a paper. The other version states a fact, so it is not an effective thesis statement.

10. a. This sentence focuses on the specific points the writer will develop in a paper. The other version, which promises a discussion of many books and films, is too broad.

Thesis statements in MLA papers 2, page 5

1. a. This statement asserts a position about the Fairness Doctrine that can be argued in a paper. The other statement is too factual to make an effective thesis.
2. a. This statement asserts a position about television that can be argued in a paper, and it previews the structure of the argument. The other statement is too vague and too broad to make an effective thesis.
3. b. This statement asserts a position and suggests a clear focus for a paper. The other statement is too broad and too unfocused to make an effective thesis.
4. b. This statement makes an assertion that can be argued with evidence in a paper. The other statement is too factual to make an effective thesis.
5. b. The other statement presents a fact, but it does not take a position on an issue, so it would not make an effective thesis.
6. a. This statement makes a claim that can be argued in a paper with evidence from the novel and other sources. The other statement is too factual and too trivial to work as a thesis.
7. a. This statement provides a proposed course of action that can be supported with evidence in a paper. The other statement is vague; it lacks a focused claim that can be argued in a paper.
8. a. This statement makes a focused assertion that can be argued with evidence in a paper. The other statement is too vague to make an effective thesis.
9. a. This statement makes a claim that can be supported with evidence in a paper. The other statement is merely factual and cannot be an effective thesis.
10. b. This statement makes an assertion that sets up a framework for a paper. The other statement is too vague to make an effective thesis.

Avoiding plagiarism in MLA papers 1, page 7

1. Plagiarized. The student uses some exact words and phrases from the source (*intimate, broken into discrete bits*) without enclosing them in quotation marks and also mimics the structure of the source.
2. OK. The student has correctly enclosed the exact words of the source in quotation marks and has used brackets for a word added to fit the surrounding sentence.
3. OK. The student has correctly enclosed the exact words of the source in quotation marks.
4. OK. The student has correctly paraphrased the source without using the language or structure of the source.
5. Plagiarized. The student has put quotation marks around exact words from the source but has failed to cite the author of the source in a signal phrase or in parentheses.

Avoiding plagiarism in MLA papers 2, page 8

1. Plagiarized. The student uses some exact words and phrases from the source (*spend more time thinking and talking about other people than . . . anything else*) without enclosing them in quotation marks and also mimics the structure of the source. The student also has not cited the source in a signal phrase or in parentheses.
2. OK. The student has correctly enclosed the exact words of the source in quotation marks and has cited the source of the quotation in parentheses.
3. OK. The student has correctly enclosed the exact words of the source in quotation marks and has cited the source of the quotations in a signal phrase and in parentheses.
4. Plagiarized. The student has put exact words from the source in quotation marks but has omitted the words *briefly but* after *themselves*, and that omission distorts the meaning of the source.
5. OK. The student has paraphrased the source's ideas without using the exact words or structure of the source and has cited the source in a signal phrase and in parentheses.

Avoiding plagiarism in MLA papers 3, page 9

1. Plagiarized. Although the source is cited, the student has paraphrased the source too closely. Simply changing a word or two and switching the order of phrases is not acceptable. A paraphrase must be in the writer's own words.
2. Plagiarized. The student has paraphrased the source too closely by borrowing the sentence structure of the original and then plugging in synonyms (*disseminate* for *spreads out*, *pervade* for *permeate*).
3. OK. In addition to providing a citation, the student has paraphrased the source without borrowing language from the source.
4. OK. In addition to providing a citation, the student has enclosed exact language from the source in quotation marks.
5. Plagiarized. Although the source is cited, the student has paraphrased the source too closely and borrowed language from the source (*far-reaching popularity*, for example) without enclosing it in quotation marks.
6. OK. In addition to providing a citation, the student has paraphrased the source without borrowing language from the source.
7. Plagiarized. In addition to copying from the source almost word-for-word without using quotation marks, the student has failed to cite the author and page number for the source.
8. OK. In addition to providing a signal phrase naming the author and a page number in parentheses, the student has enclosed the source's exact language in quotation marks.
9. Plagiarized. The student has paraphrased the source too closely, has not enclosed borrowed language in quotation marks, and has not given the author and page number.
10. OK. In addition to providing a citation, the student has enclosed exact language from the source in quotation marks.

Avoiding plagiarism in MLA papers 4, page 11

1. Plagiarized. The student uses language borrowed from the original source without quotation marks and without crediting the author. The following is an acceptable revision:
   Rushdie points out that "the sheer number of occasions on which people cry" in *The Wizard of Oz* is astounding (223).
2. OK. The student has paraphrased without using language or structure from the source. The student also cites the author's name and gives the page numbers for the source in parentheses.
3. Plagiarized. The student has borrowed words from the source without putting them in quotation marks (*tears of frustration, sodden with tears, rusts up again*) and has plugged in synonyms for other language from the source (*cries* for *bawls, hits* for *bops*).
4. OK. The student has correctly placed borrowed language in quotation marks and given the author's name and the page numbers on which the quotation can be found.
5. Plagiarized. The student has used the words *extreme performance* from the source without putting them in quotation marks.

Avoiding plagiarism in MLA papers 5, page 12

1. OK. The student has enclosed the exact words from the source in quotation marks and identifies the author in a signal phrase and the page number in parentheses.
2. OK. The student has paraphrased the source without using its language or structure and has credited the author and cited the page number on which the ideas can be found.
3. Plagiarized. Although the student has credited the source with a signal phrase and a page number in parentheses, the student paraphrases the source too closely, using the same or similar words (*seldom, stick, faithfully, wander*) and borrowing the sentence structure from the source.
4. Plagiarized. The student's paraphrase uses language from the source without quotation marks (*irrelevancies, embarrassed, relevancy*) and a sentence structure that is too close to that in the source. In addition, the student does not credit the author of the ideas or the page number on which they can be found.
5. Plagiarized. The student has used language from the source (*modern ears, wandered all around and arrived nowhere*) without enclosing it in quotation marks.

Recognizing common knowledge in MLA papers, page 13

1. Common knowledge. Yoknapatawpha County is mentioned in virtually all sources discussing Faulkner, so his invention of this place can be considered common knowledge.
2. Needs citation. The scholar whose research led to this hypothesis should be given credit.
3. Common knowledge. Information about birth and death dates and the life circumstances of well-known authors usually does not require citation.
4. Needs citation. A reader would not encounter this information repeatedly in books and articles on Shakespeare, so it requires a citation.
5. Needs citation. This information might be considered controversial, especially among admirers of Disney.
6. Common knowledge. This is information that would appear in many sources on Wordsworth and Shelley, so a paper on these poets would not need to cite it.
7. Needs citation. Statistics generally require a citation.
8. Common knowledge. This is a definition of a standard literary form—a type of information found in almost any introductory literature text.
9. Common knowledge. This information about Iris Murdoch is widely known, and a student would find mention of it in most recent sources related to Murdoch.
10. Needs citation. This information would probably be surprising to many readers (and some might doubt its veracity), so a citation is needed.

Integrating sources in MLA papers 1, page 14

1. This sentence is unacceptable. Although the student has used quotation marks around the exact words of the source, the student has failed to use an ellipsis mark to indicate missing words from the source (*and trumpets*).
2. This sentence is unacceptable. It is an acceptable paraphrase of the source's ideas, but the student has failed to cite the author of the source either in a signal phrase or in parentheses.
3. OK. The student has used quotation marks around words taken directly from the source. The student also has inserted the word *that* in brackets to make the quotation fit grammatically with the surrounding sentence.
4. OK. The student has used quotation marks around words taken directly from the source and has indicated the author of the source in parentheses.
5. This sentence is unacceptable. The student has used quotation marks around words taken directly from the source but has failed to cite the author of the source either in a signal phrase or in parentheses.

Integrating sources in MLA papers 2, page 15

1. The sentence is unacceptable. The student has failed to enclose borrowed language in quotation marks and to introduce the quoted words with a signal phrase naming the authors. The following is an acceptable revision:
   Burrows and Wallace note that the Delmonico brothers' French restaurant was among the first eating establishments "to let diners order from a menu of choices, at any time they pleased, and sit at their own cloth-covered tables" (437).
2. OK. Quoted words appear in quotation marks, and the student has provided a context for the quotation and named the authors in a signal phrase.
3. OK. The student has enclosed exact words from the source in quotation marks and has introduced the quotation with a signal phrase naming the authors.
4. This passage is unacceptable. The second sentence is a dropped quotation. The student has failed to provide a signal phrase naming the authors. The following is an acceptable revision:
   In 1830, the Delmonico brothers opened one of the first restaurants in New York City. "This was a sharp break," according to Burrows and Wallace, "from the fixed fare and simultaneous seatings at common hotel tables—so crowded (one guidebook warned) that your elbows were 'pinned down to your sides like the wings of a trussed fowl'" (437).
5. This sentence is unacceptable. The words enclosed in quotation marks are not word-for-word accurate. The following is an acceptable revision:
   According to Burrows and Wallace, the Delmonico brothers' original shop enticed New Yorkers "with a half-dozen pine tables where customers could sample fine French pastries, coffee, chocolate, wine, and liquor" (437).
6. OK. The student has enclosed words from the source in quotation marks, and the word *such* (added to make the student's sentence grammatical) appears in brackets to indicate that it does not occur in the original source.
7. This passage is unacceptable. The student has borrowed words from the source without enclosing them in quotation marks. The following is an acceptable revision:
   Burrows and Wallace observe that the Delmonico brothers' restaurant first attracted "resident European agents of export houses, who felt themselves marooned among a people with barbarous eating habits" (437).

8. This sentence is unacceptable. Although the student has enclosed exact language from the source in quotation marks, the student has failed to introduce the quotation with a signal phrase naming the authors. The following is an acceptable revision:
   Burrows and Wallace observe that the Delmonico brothers' restaurant first attracted "resident European agents of export houses, who felt themselves marooned among a people with barbarous eating habits" (437).
9. OK. The student has enclosed words from the source in quotation marks and indicated changes in the original with brackets and an ellipsis mark.
10. This passage is unacceptable. The second sentence is a dropped quotation. The student has failed to provide a signal phrase naming the authors. The following is an acceptable revision:
    Native New Yorkers were at first suspicious of the concept of a restaurant. But as Burrows and Wallace note, "The idea soon caught on, . . . more restaurants appeared, and harried businessmen abandoned the ancient practice of going home for lunch" (437).

Integrating sources in MLA papers 3, page 17

1. This sentence is unacceptable. The second part of the sentence is a direct quotation from the source, so it must appear in quotation marks:
   Wind power accounts for more than 1% of California's electricity, reports Frederic Golden, and "[d]uring breezy early mornings in summer, the contribution goes even higher" (B1).
2. OK. Quoted words appear in quotation marks, and the student provides the author's name in the signal phrase and the page number in parentheses.
3. This passage is unacceptable. The words appearing in quotation marks are not word-for-word accurate. Also, the statement is not accurate because the 8% figure applies only on certain days. The following is an acceptable revision:
   Mary A. Ilyin reports that under certain weather conditions, "the wind accounts for up to 8%" of California's electricity (qtd. in Golden B1).
4. OK. The brackets indicate that the word *California's* does not appear in the original source, and otherwise the quotation is word-for-word accurate. In addition, the MLA citation correctly indicates that the words belong to Ilyin, who was quoted by Golden.
5. This passage is unacceptable. The second sentence is a dropped quotation. Quotations must be introduced with a signal phrase, usually naming the author. The following is an acceptable revision:
   California has pioneered the use of wind power. According to Frederic Golden, "Half of California's turbines . . . are located in Altamont Pass" (B1).

Integrating sources in MLA papers 4, page 18

1. OK. The student has put quotation marks around the exact words from the source and has handled the MLA citation correctly, putting the name of the author in a signal phrase and the page number in parentheses.
2. The sentence is unacceptable. The phrase *active safety* is enclosed in quotation marks in the source; single quotation marks are required for a quotation within a quotation. In addition, the student has failed to use an ellipsis mark to indicate that the word *which* is omitted from the quotation. The following is an acceptable revision:
   Gladwell argues that "'active safety' . . . is every bit as important" as a vehicle's ability to withstand a collision (31).

3. This passage is unacceptable. The second sentence is a dropped quotation. Quotations should be introduced with a signal phrase, usually naming the author. The following is an acceptable revision:

>A majority of drivers can, indeed, be wrong. As Malcolm Gladwell points out, "Most of us think that S.U.V.s are much safer than sports cars" (31).

4. OK. The student has introduced the quotation with a signal phrase and used brackets to indicate the change from *you* to *they* to fit the grammar of the sentence.

5. This sentence is unacceptable. The student has changed the wording of the source (*of surviving*) to fit the grammar of the sentence (*to survive*) but has not indicated the change with brackets. The following is an acceptable revision:

>Gladwell explains that most people expect an SUV "[to survive] a collision with a hypothetical tractor-trailer in the other lane" (31).

MLA documentation: in-text citations 1, page 19

1. a. Because Sommers is quoted in an article written by someone else, MLA style requires the abbreviation "qtd. in" (for "quoted in") before the author of the article in the in-text citation.

2. b. When the author of a source is given in a signal phrase, the title of the source is not necessary in an in-text citation.

3. b. For a work with three or more authors, the first author's name is used but "et al." is used for all other names.

4. a. Statistics used from a source must be cited with author and page number.

5. b. The author's name, not the title of the source, should be used in an in-text citation.

6. a. The exact words of the source are enclosed in quotation marks.

7. b. For an unsigned source, a shortened form of the title is used in the in-text citation.

8. a. When the works cited list includes two or more works by one author, the in-text citation includes a shortened form of the title of the work cited.

9. b. A website with no author should be cited by a shortened form of the title, not by the sponsor of the website.

10. a. For a source with two authors, both authors should be given in the in-text citation.

MLA documentation: in-text citations 2, page 23

1. b. If two works by the same author are included in the works cited list, the in-text citation must give a shortened form of the title of the work cited in addition to the author's name.

2. a. In MLA style for a source with two authors, both authors' names are given in the signal phrase.

3. a. When two or more works are cited in the same parentheses, the authors' names are separated by a semicolon.

4. a. For an unpaginated article from a website, no page number is given in the in-text citation, and the title of the article is not given in parentheses.

5. b. For a work in an anthology, only the name of the author of the selection should be given in the in-text citation. The name of the editor is not given.

6. b. Grigoriadis is quoting Starland, so the parenthetical citation includes the abbreviation "qtd. in" to indicate that the words are not Grigoriadis's.

7. a. The in-text citation for a newspaper article includes the exact page number on which the quotation appears.

8. a. For an online source with no page numbers, a parenthetical citation naming the author of the work is sufficient in MLA style.

9. b. In MLA style, a work with no author should be cited with a shortened form of the title.

10. b. A work with no author is cited by a shortened form of the title in an MLA in-text citation.

MLA documentation: in-text citations 3, page 27

1. a. The author's name is given in the signal phrase, and the page number is given in the parenthetical citation. The article title is not needed in the citation.

2. a. The citation names the author of the work being quoted, not the editor of the book.

3. a. When a long quotation is indented in MLA style, quotation marks are not used to enclose the quotation; the parenthetical citation comes after the end punctuation of the quotation.

4. b. When the works cited list includes two works by the same author, the citation includes the title (or a shortened form of the title) of the work.

5. a. The signal phrase (*Mayer claims . . .*) names the author of the essay; the editors of the anthology are not given in the in-text citation.

6. b. For unpaginated material from a website, a signal phrase naming the author of the work is sufficient in an MLA in-text citation.

7. a. When a work has two authors, both names are given in the in-text citation.

8. b. When a source has a known author, the author is included in the signal phrase or in a parenthetical citation. (Page numbers are not given because the work is from an unpaginated online source.)

9. a. Because Twain's words appear in an article written by someone else (a secondary source), the abbreviation "qtd. in" is used in the parenthetical citation before the author of the secondary source.

10. a. Both authors' names are included in the parenthetical citation. (A page number is not required in this citation because the article was accessed in a database that does not show page breaks.)

MLA documentation: identifying elements of sources, page 31

1. a. The author of the internal page, "Willa Cather: A Brief Biographical Sketch," is Amy Ahearn. Andrew Jewell is the editor of the *Willa Cather Archive* website.

2. b. The copyright notice at the bottom of the home page states that the website was updated in January 2017. If the month is listed in addition to the year, the month should be included in the citation.

3. b. An MLA works cited entry for a journal requires the abbreviations for volume, number, and pages as well as the season if one is given in the source.

4. a. The works cited entry should begin with the author of the article, not with the subject.

5. b. In the title of a book in MLA style, only the principal words (nouns, pronouns, adjectives, and verbs) are capitalized, regardless of the capitalization that appears on the title page.

6. b. MLA style does not require the place of publication.

7. a. The abbreviation "P" (for "Press") is used only for a university press. The word is spelled out in other publishers' names.

8. b. This podcast is an interview, so both the interviewer and the interviewee are named along with the title of the podcast.

9. b. As author of the essay you are citing, Baudrillard would appear first in the works cited entry.
10. b. The city of publication is not included in a works cited entry for a book.

MLA documentation: works cited 1, page 37

1. b. A works cited entry for a journal should include the volume and issue numbers in addition to the date.
2. b. In MLA style, a work with three or more authors is listed by the name of the first author followed by "et al." (Latin for "and others").
3. a. The page number is not used in a works cited entry for a book.
4. a. Because the student has used dialogue from the film and has not emphasized one person's contribution, the MLA works cited entry begins with the title of the film, not the director's name.
5. a. The sponsor of a news site is not included if the name is the same as or similar to the title of the site.
6. a. The names of university presses should be abbreviated, with "UP" standing for "University Press."
7. a. A works cited entry for a review should give the author of the work reviewed as well as the title.
8. b. The MLA works cited entry for an online article includes the entire URL of the source.
9. b. The date is in the proper order and the month is abbreviated.
10. a. In MLA style, when the author of a work is unknown, the works cited entry begins with the work's title. The term "Anonymous" is not used.

MLA documentation: works cited 2, page 41

1. a. The publisher's name is given in full.
2. a. In an MLA works cited entry, the names of all months except May, June, and July are abbreviated.
3. b. When a works cited list contains more than one source by the same author, the works are listed alphabetically, with the author's name given in the first entry and three hyphens in place of the author's name in subsequent entries. This is the second entry, so three hyphens appear in place of the author's name.
4. b. The author's name is given last name first.
5. a. Because the student has quoted from the foreword of the book, the foreword and its author are given first in the MLA works cited entry.
6. b. The works cited entry for an online video includes the complete URL for the source.
7. a. An MLA works cited entry for a part of a work, such as a chapter, includes the page numbers on which the part of the work appears.
8. b. If the sponsor's name is the same as or similar to the title of the website, the sponsor's name should be omitted.
9. b. Because the student has used dialogue from the film and has not emphasized one person's contribution, the MLA works cited entry begins with the title of the film, not the director's name.
10. a. An MLA works cited entry for a review includes the author and title of the review along with relevant information about the work being reviewed.

MLA documentation: works cited 3, page 45

1. b. An MLA works cited entry for an article with no author begins with the title of the article.
2. b. The terms "volume" and "number" are abbreviated, and the name of the database and the URL for the database home page are included.

3. a. When citing a single work from an anthology, the individual work is listed first, beginning with its author's name.
4. b. If a newspaper article appears on pages that are not consecutive, the first page number is followed by a plus sign.
5. a. In an MLA works cited entry, the publication date appears after the website title.
6. a. A works cited entry for an interview begins with the name of the person interviewed, not the person who conducted the interview.
7. b. Elements following the title are separated by commas. "Narrated by" is also spelled out.
8. a. The translator's name is given after the title of the work.
9. a. The access date is not given because the website has an update date.
10. b. A work from a website includes the URL for the work.

MLA documentation, page 48

1. False. A URL is never used in an in-text citation.
2. True. The alphabetical organization helps readers quickly find the source that has been cited in the text.
3. False. A list of works cited must give complete publication information for any sources cited in the paper. In-text citations alone are not sufficient.
4. True. MLA provides an option for including the author's name: It can appear in a signal phrase or in parentheses.
5. False. When a work's author is unknown, the work is listed under its title.
6. False. In the works cited list, only the first author is listed in reverse order (last name first). A second author is listed in normal order (first name first).
7. True. If the author is named in a signal phrase, it is possible that nothing will appear in parentheses.
8. False. MLA style does not use any abbreviation before the page number in an in-text citation.
9. True. Because more than one work will appear in the works cited list, the title is necessary for identifying the exact work that has been cited. The author's name is not enough.
10. True. When a permalink or a DOI is available, use that instead of a URL in the works cited list.

Thesis statements in APA papers 1, page 49

1. b. This sentence asserts a specific cause and effect that can be developed into an argument. The other sentence is a vague prediction that would be difficult to support with scientific evidence.
2. a. This sentence provides an assertion and specific details that the writer can develop to support the assertion. The other sentence is too vague.
3. a. This sentence suggests that the paper will examine reasons for police reluctance to adopt a new system. The other sentence is too vague to be an acceptable thesis.
4. b. This sentence offers an assertion that can be developed into an argument. The other sentence simply states a fact.
5. a. This sentence presents an idea that can be argued in a paper. The other sentence simply lists symptoms of a disorder.
6. b. This sentence focuses on a causal connection between images and eating disorders. The other sentence is too broad to develop in depth.
7. b. This sentence offers an assertion that a paper can argue. The other sentence simply states a fact.
8. a. This sentence focuses on specific causes that can be discussed in a paper. The other sentence is too vague.
9. a. This sentence focuses on one quality and provides several ideas that the writer can develop in an essay. The other sentence is too broad.

10. b. This sentence makes a clear and specific assertion about an arguable matter. The other sentence is too broad.

Thesis statements in APA papers 2, page 51

1. b. This statement makes an assertion about homeschooling that can be developed in a paper. The other statement is a statistic; it is too factual to be an effective thesis.
2. a. This statement makes an assertion about the child care industry that can be supported with evidence in a paper. The other statement is too vague to be an effective thesis.
3. b. This statement takes a position on gambling revenues that can be argued in a paper. The other statement is too factual to be an effective thesis.
4. a. This statement makes an assertion about the validity of one particular theory, and this assertion can be argued in a paper. The other statement is too factual to be an effective thesis.
5. a. This statement makes a focused assertion that can be supported with evidence in a paper. It also suggests a counterargument that the writer can develop. The other statement contains several facts but does not provide an assertion that can be developed in a paper.
6. b. This statement makes a claim based on "recent evidence," setting up a paper that can discuss this evidence and argue a position. The other sentence merely states a fact about what "most American parents" want and would not make an effective thesis.
7. b. This statement is a call to action; it makes an assertion about suicide rates that can be argued in a paper. The other statement makes a claim that is too vague to be an effective thesis.
8. a. This statement makes a focused claim about standardized tests that can be supported with evidence in a paper. The other statement would not make an effective thesis because it lacks focus and assertiveness; it broadly summarizes two opposing viewpoints on NCLB without taking a stand on either one.
9. b. This statement makes an assertion about teacher salaries that can be supported with evidence in a paper. The other statement is too factual to be an effective thesis.
10. a. This statement is a call to action; it makes an assertion about the need for violence prevention programs for military families that can be argued in a paper. The other statement makes a claim that is too factual to be an effective thesis.

Avoiding plagiarism in APA papers 1, page 53

1. Plagiarized. The student mimics the structure of the source's sentence and uses synonyms that are too close to the source's language (*in control at times* for *sometimes . . . in control*).
2. OK. The student paraphrases the source's ideas and includes the direct words of the source in quotation marks.
3. Plagiarized. The student uses some exact phrases from the source (*conscious mind avatar*, *what people to associate with*, *what to believe*, and *what to do*) without enclosing them in quotation marks.
4. OK. The student has correctly enclosed the exact words of the source in quotation marks and has used an ellipsis mark for words omitted from the source.
5. Plagiarized. The student uses some of the source's exact words without enclosing them in quotation marks and also paraphrases the source too closely.
6. OK. The student has correctly enclosed the exact words of the source in quotation marks.
7. Plagiarized. The student uses the source's exact words (*whether those choices are freely willed*) without enclosing all of them in quotation marks.

8. Plagiarized. While the student paraphrases without using words or structure from the source, the student has failed to cite the author, date, and page number of the source.
9. OK. The student paraphrases without using words or structure from the source.
10. OK. The student has placed the source's exact words in quotation marks.

Avoiding plagiarism in APA papers 2, page 55

1. Plagiarized. Although the student has cited the author, date, and page number for the source, the student has used the exact words of the source without quotation marks. The following is an acceptable revision:
   According to a report by the Pew Charitable Trusts (2010), prison is "an increasingly predictable destination" for men—especially for black men (p. 8).
2. OK. The student has put the source's exact words in quotation marks and has introduced the quoted language with a signal phrase.
3. Plagiarized. The student has dropped the data into the text without naming the author and listing the date of publication either in a signal phrase or in parentheses. The following is an acceptable revision:
   Research has shown that 1 in 57 young white males (20 to 34 years old) is in prison and that the rate for young white males of the same age *without* a high school diploma increases significantly—to 1 in 8 (Pew Charitable Trusts, 2010, p. 8).
4. Plagiarized. The student has not cited the author or the date of the source. The following is an acceptable revision:
   Data in a Pew Charitable Trusts report (2010) reveal that when black men fail to complete high school, by the time they are 20 or 30 years old jail looks more and more likely (p. 8).
5. OK. The student has put the source's exact words in quotation marks and has integrated the quoted language effectively into the existing sentence.

Avoiding plagiarism in APA papers 3, page 57

1. Plagiarized. The student has copied chunks of text from the source word-for-word without enclosing the borrowed words in quotation marks and without providing a citation.
2. Plagiarized. Although the student has cited the source, the paraphrase is too close to the structure and language of the original.
3. OK. In addition to citing the source, the student has enclosed exact words from the source in quotation marks.
4. OK. In addition to citing the source, the student has enclosed exact words from the source in quotation marks.
5. OK. In addition to citing the source, the student has paraphrased it without borrowing too much of its language.
6. Plagiarized. Although a borrowed phrase correctly appears in quotation marks, the student has paraphrased the source too closely, borrowing structure from the original and plugging in synonyms (*ill* for *sick*, *not at all what you would expect in* for *quite different from*, *ailment* for *illness*).
7. Plagiarized. Although the sentence begins as an acceptable paraphrase, it ends by using the source almost word-for-word without quotation marks.
8. OK. In addition to citing the source, the student has paraphrased it without borrowing too much of its language.
9. Plagiarized. In addition to copying the source almost word-for-word without using quotation marks, the student has failed to cite the author, year, and page number for the source.
10. OK. In addition to citing the source, the student has paraphrased it without borrowing too much of its language.

Avoiding plagiarism in APA papers 4, page 59

1. Plagiarized. Although the student has correctly cited the source, the student has failed to enclose in quotation marks all the words taken from the source. The following is an acceptable revision:

   Diamond (2004) explained that the 11 territories on Easter Island were "loosely integrated religiously, economically, and politically under the leadership of one paramount chief" (p. 8).
2. OK. The student has paraphrased the source without using language or structure from the source. The student also has used a parenthetical citation in proper APA style.
3. OK. The student has enclosed exact words from the source in quotation marks and has cited the quotation properly in APA style.
4. Plagiarized. The student has borrowed the sentence structure of the source and has substituted synonyms for many words (*status* for *prestige*, *island-to-island endeavors* for *inter-island efforts*, for instance).
5. Plagiarized. The student has used exact words from the source without enclosing them in quotation marks and has failed to cite the page number from which the words were borrowed. The following is an acceptable revision:

   Diamond (2004) noted that rather than compete with chiefs on other Polynesian islands, Easter Island's chiefs competed among themselves "by erecting statues representing their high-ranking ancestors" (p. 8).

Recognizing common knowledge in APA papers, page 60

1. Needs citation. The results of a scientific study such as the trial of a drug should be cited.
2. Common knowledge. This fact was reported in media sources in 2012 with great regularity; it can be considered common knowledge.
3. Needs citation. Although readers may have anecdotal evidence of the popularity of particular baby names, certain knowledge of the number-one name generally requires investigation. The source should be cited.
4. Needs citation. This information is probably known only to specialists. The source should be cited.
5. Common knowledge. An awareness of the connection between taste and smell is common; many people have noticed how a temporary loss of the sense of smell affects the ability to taste.
6. Needs citation. While the existence of the Homestead Act might be considered common knowledge, the statistical fact that women filed 10% of the claims must be cited.
7. Common knowledge. This fact is widely known even outside of the field of baseball (or sports). Information about major records in sports is found in many different sources.
8. Common knowledge. This information is mentioned in most discussions of earthquakes and California. It is a well-known fact that does not require citation.
9. Needs citation. Information that presents the findings of a study—particularly findings that go against the prevailing wisdom—should be cited.
10. Common knowledge. This information can be found in any number of sources, so it does not need a citation.

Integrating sources in APA papers 1, page 61

1. OK. The student has paraphrased the source's ideas, has used a signal phrase to give credit to the source, and has cited the page numbers on which the ideas can be found.
2. This sentence is unacceptable. Although the student has cited the author, date, and page number for the source,

the student has used exact words from the source (*takes 2.2 calories of fossil fuel, 40 calories to produce one calorie of beef protein*) without enclosing them in quotation marks and has failed to provide a signal phrase introducing the quotations. The following is an acceptable revision:

   According to Bittman (2009), it "takes 2.2 calories of fossil fuel" to produce one calorie of edible corn, while it takes "40 calories to produce one calorie of beef protein" (p. 16).
3. OK. The student has paraphrased the source's ideas and has used a signal phrase to give credit to the source.
4. OK. The student has enclosed language from the source in quotation marks and has correctly incorporated the quotation into the sentence.
5. This sentence is unacceptable. The student has enclosed language from the source in quotation marks, but the student should have used an ellipsis mark to indicate that the words between the dashes have been omitted. The following is an acceptable revision:

   Bittman (2009) explained that "if you process that corn, and feed it to a steer, and take into account all the other needs that steer has through its lifetime . . . you're responsible for 40 calories of energy to get the same calorie of protein" (pp. 16-17).
6. OK. The student has paraphrased the source's ideas and has used a signal phrase to give credit to the source.
7. This sentence is unacceptable. Although the student has cited the author, date, and page number for the source, the student has paraphrased the source too closely, substituting synonyms (*every* for *each*, *using* for *consuming*) but keeping the same sentence structure. The following is an acceptable revision:

   Bittman (2009) argued against raising livestock, urging readers to be mindful of the significantly higher energy consumption required (p. 17).
8. This passage is unacceptable. The student has cited the author, date, and page numbers for the quotation but has dropped the quotation into the text without using a signal phrase. The following is an acceptable revision:

   Raising livestock takes more energy than does raising vegetables, Bittman (2009) argues. "If you process . . . corn, and feed it to a steer, and take into account all the other needs that steer has through its lifetime — land use, chemical fertilizers (largely petroleum-based), pesticides, machinery, transport, drugs, water, and so on — you're responsible for 40 calories of energy to get the same calorie of protein" (pp. 16-17).
9. OK. The student has used quotation marks around words taken directly from the source and has used brackets to indicate a word changed slightly to fit into the surrounding sentence.
10. This passage is unacceptable. The student has cited the author, date, and page number for the source but has written part paraphrase and part quotation and included them both in the quotation marks. The following is an acceptable revision:

    In terms of fossil-fuel usage, Bittman (2009) compared the energy required to raise a steer for food consumption to the gasoline used in driving two coast-to-coast round trips in an energy-efficient car (p. 17).

Integrating sources in APA papers 2, page 63

1. This sentence is not acceptable. The student has used quotation marks around words from the source, but in omitting the words *women they interview*, the student has changed

the meaning of the quotation to be broader than the writer intended. The following is an acceptable revision:

> Bianchi (2013) cited research from Edin and Kefalas, which argued that marriage "has great symbolic value among the poor women" in the study (p. 326).

2. OK. The student has paraphrased the source's ideas and has used a signal phrase to give credit to the source.

3. This passage is unacceptable. The student has dropped the quotation into the text without using a signal phrase naming the author. The following is an acceptable revision:

> Bianchi (2013) pointed out that women living in poverty "hope to marry and they want a stable two-parent family and all its trappings as much as their more advantaged peers" (p. 326).

4. OK. The student has enclosed language from the source in quotation marks and has correctly incorporated the quotations into the wording of the surrounding sentence.

5. This sentence is not acceptable. The student has enclosed language from the source in quotation marks, but the student should have used an ellipsis mark to indicate that the words *on a number of dimensions—trusted* have been omitted. The following is an acceptable revision:

> Bianchi (2013) noted that the women interviewed need to know that men "can be trusted . . . to put the interests of family first" and can lead stable lives (p. 326).

Integrating sources in APA papers 3, page 64

1. This sentence is not acceptable. The student has enclosed language from the source in quotation marks, but the student should have used an ellipsis mark to indicate that some words (*which correlate closely with IQ*) have been omitted.

2. This passage is unacceptable. The student has dropped the quotation into the text without using a signal phrase naming the author. The following is an acceptable revision:

> Most GED recipients did not continue their education after receiving their certificates. Tough (2012) noted that "at age twenty-two, . . . just 3 percent of GED recipients were enrolled in a four-year university" (p. xviii).

3. OK. The student has enclosed language from the source in quotation marks and has correctly incorporated the quotation into the wording of the surrounding sentence.

4. OK. The student has paraphrased the source's ideas and has used a signal phrase to give credit to the source.

5. This sentence is unacceptable. Although the student has cited the author, date, and page number for the source, the student has used exact words from the source (*are, on average, considerably more intelligent than high-school dropouts*) without enclosing them in quotation marks.

Integrating sources in APA papers 4, page 65

1. This sentence is unacceptable. Although the student has cited the author, date, and page number for the source, the student has used the exact words of the source without quotation marks. The following is an acceptable revision:

> Researchers at Utrecht University found that bereaved spouses "who often talked with others and briefly wrote in diaries about their emotions fared no better than their tight-lipped, unexpressive counterparts" (Bower, 2002, p. 131).

2. This sentence is unacceptable. Although the student has used quotation marks and has cited the source correctly, the student has omitted words from the source (*about their emotions*) without using the ellipsis mark. The following is an acceptable revision:

> Researchers at Utrecht University found that bereaved spouses "who often talked with others and briefly wrote in diaries . . . fared no better than their tight-lipped, unexpressive counterparts" (Bower, 2002, p. 131).

3. OK. The student has put the source's exact words in quotation marks and has used the ellipsis mark to indicate that some words from the source have been omitted.

4. This sentence is unacceptable. The quotation is not word-for-word accurate from the source: The student has changed *have long theorized* to *have always believed* and *the death of a loved one* to *a loved one's death*. The following is an acceptable revision:

> According to Bower (2002), "Mental-health workers have long theorized that it takes grueling emotional exertion to recover from the death of a loved one" (p. 131).

5. This passage is unacceptable. The student has dropped the quotation into the text without using a signal phrase naming the author. The following is an acceptable revision:

> Mental health professionals have assumed that people stricken by grief need a great deal of help. Bower (2002) pointed out that "so-called grief work, now the stock-in-trade of a growing number of grief counselors, entails confronting the reality of a loved one's demise and grappling with the harsh emotions triggered by that loss" (p. 131).

Note that it is acceptable to change the capital *S* to lowercase at the beginning of the quotation to fit the grammar of the student's sentence.

6. OK. The student has introduced the quotation with a signal phrase naming the author and giving the date in parentheses and has placed the exact words from the source in quotation marks.

7. OK. The student has enclosed language from the source in quotation marks and has used brackets to indicate that words from the source have been changed to fit the grammar of the student's sentence (*confronting* changed to *confront*, *grappling* changed to *grapple*).

8. This sentence is unacceptable. In APA style, the verb in a signal phrase should be in the past or the past perfect tense (*found* or *have found*), not the present tense (*find*). The following is an acceptable revision:

> Researchers at Utrecht University have found no difference in the speed of adapting to a spouse's death among subjects "who often talked with others and briefly wrote in diaries" and "their tight-lipped, unexpressive counterparts" (Bower, 2002, p. 131).

9. This passage is unacceptable. Although the student has used a correct APA-style signal phrase and has put the page number in parentheses following the quotation, the student should not have used quotation marks to enclose a long quotation that is set off from the text by indenting. The following is an acceptable revision:

> Bower (2002) noted that new studies may change the common perception of how people recover from grief: Among bereaved spouses tracked for up to 2 years after their partners' death, those who often talked with others and briefly wrote in diaries about their emotions fared no better than their tight-lipped, unexpressive counterparts, according to psychologist Margaret Stroebe of Utrecht University in the Netherlands and her colleagues. (p. 131)

10. OK. The student has enclosed borrowed language in quotation marks and has used an ellipsis mark to indicate that the word *however* has been omitted from the source. The student also has used a proper APA signal phrase and parenthetical citation.

APA documentation: in-text citations 1, page 67

1. a. The date is given in parentheses following the author's name, and the page number for the quotation is given in parentheses following the quotation.
2. a. For a work with three authors, all authors' names are given in the parentheses at the first mention.
3. b. In APA style, the abbreviation "p." is used with the page number in the parentheses.
4. b. In APA style, the page number is given after the paraphrase. Only a date is included in the parentheses following the authors' names.
5. b. The person interviewed is the only person cited in the parentheses, and the date follows the interviewee's name.
6. a. The page number follows the quotation in parentheses.
7. a. The date follows the author's name. No page number follows the quotation; APA style does not use the abbreviation "n.p."
8. a. For a work with six or more authors, only the first author's name is given, followed by "et al.," in an in-text citation.
9. b. The date in parentheses follows the author's name in the in-text citation.
10. a. The date follows the author's name in the in-text citation, even for a paraphrase from an unpaginated source.

APA documentation: in-text citations 2, page 71

1. a. For a source quoted in another source, the words "as cited in" are used in the parenthetical citation.
2. b. For a work with six or more authors, only the first author's name, followed by "et al.," is used in the in-text citation, and the date is given in parentheses following the author's name.
3. b. The date follows the author's name in parentheses, and the page number follows the quotation.
4. a. Both the figure number and the page on which it is found are in the parenthetical citation following the quotation.
5. a. Only the author's last name, without an initial, is used in the in-text citation.
6. a. For a source quoted in another source, the words "as cited in" are used in the parenthetical citation. Even with this language, the author *and* date must still be included.
7. a. An unpaginated source needs only the author's name and the date in the parenthetical citation. APA style does not use the abbreviation "n.p."
8. a. Only the author's name and the date, in parentheses following the name, are required for a source from the web. The name of the website is not used.
9. b. For the second reference to a source with four authors, only the first author's name and the abbreviation "et al." are used in the in-text citation.
10. b. An abbreviation for a corporate author is appropriate in references after the first.

APA documentation: in-text citations 3, page 75

1. b. The correct wording for a source quoted in another source is "as cited in."
2. b. For a work with two or more authors, the word "and" is used between the last two authors' names in a text sentence.
3. a. For the second reference to a source with four authors, only the first author's name and the abbreviation "et al." are used in the in-text citation.
4. b. Because this sentence includes both a paraphrase and a direct quotation, the entire span of the material paraphrased is cited in the parentheses.

5. a. An unpaginated source needs only the author's name and the date in the in-text citation. APA style does not use the abbreviation "n.p."

APA documentation: identifying elements of sources, page 77

1. a. The date of publication given is the most recent date on the copyright page.
2. b. In APA style, only the first word of the title, the first word after a colon, and proper nouns are capitalized, and the edition number follows the book title.
3. a. The name of the author of the chapter appears first in the reference list entry.
4. b. The author and title of the individual work appear first in the reference list entry. In addition, the book and chapter titles are capitalized correctly in APA style.
5. a. The author's name is given first, and the title of the article is not enclosed in quotation marks.
6. a. Both the volume number and the issue number are given because each issue begins on page 1. (The year follows the author's name, not the volume number.)
7. b. If a database record contains a DOI (digital object identifier), the DOI is sufficient at the end of a reference list entry.
8. b. In APA style, the title of a blog post is not italicized. The label "Blog post" is included in brackets following the title of the post.
9. b. The term "Insights" is a title for the section of the magazine and is not part of the article title.
10. a. In an APA reference list entry for a monthly magazine, the month, the year, and the volume number are included. The issue number is included when each issue of the magazine begins on page 1, as in this case.

APA documentation: reference list 1, page 83

1. a. For an article in an online magazine, the home page of the magazine, not the direct URL for the article, is given in the reference list.
2. a. In the reference list in APA style, only the first word in a title and subtitle are capitalized.
3. b. The title "Director" and the date are in separate parentheses following the director's name. And the retrieval statement contains only the URL, not the name of the service.
4. b. APA style requires the state name (abbreviated) along with the city of publication.
5. b. For an anthology (collection) with no editors, the word "In" is followed by the title of the anthology. The abbreviation "No Ed." is not used.
6. a. When an article has a DOI, that number should appear at the end of the reference list entry.
7. a. The URL for the journal's home page, not the URL for the article, is used for an article in an online journal.
8. a. The complete date (including month and day) are given with the year for a newspaper article.
9. a. For a radio report accessed online, the URL for the online source, not the name of the network, should appear at the end of the reference list entry.
10. a. For an article retrieved from a database, if the article does not have a DOI, the URL of the journal's home page should appear at the end of the reference list entry.

APA documentation: reference list 2, page 87

1. a. When a government agency or another organization serves as both the author and the publisher, the publisher is given as "Author" in the APA reference list entry.

2. b. When an advertisement is cited in an APA reference entry, the word "Advertisement" (not the type of product) appears in brackets after the product name.
3. a. An APA reference list entry for an article in an online newspaper ends with the URL for the home page of the newspaper.
4. b. When a source has eight or more authors, the first six authors are listed, followed by three ellipsis dots and the last author's name.
5. b. In APA reference lists, page numbers are not included for citations to books.
6. a. When no DOI is available for a journal article accessed in a database, the URL for the journal's home page is included in the APA reference list entry.
7. a. APA reference list entries for articles in scholarly journals list only the year (not the season, month, or day) in parentheses.
8. a. The label "Audio podcast" follows the title of the podcast in brackets.
9. b. In an APA reference list entry for an online video file that is not dated, the abbreviation "n.d." (for "no date") is placed in parentheses.
10. b. In an APA reference list entry for a published interview, the person being interviewed is listed first, and the interviewer is named in brackets after the title of the article.

APA documentation: reference list 3, page 91

1. a. The reference list entry for a work with no author begins with the title of the work.
2. b. In APA reference entries, the identification of the main contributor—in this case "Producer/director"—appears in parentheses after the name of the contributor.
3. a. The abbreviation "p." is used before the page number of a newspaper article.
4. a. An APA reference entry for a journal article includes the page range of the article, not only the page cited in the paper.
5. a. The abbreviation "Eds." (for "Editors") is included after the editors' names in APA reference entries.
6. b. When a DOI is available for an article accessed in a database, the DOI only (not the database name) is included in an APA reference list entry.
7. a. APA reference list entries for articles in scholarly journals list only the year (not the season, month, or day) in parentheses.
8. b. For an audio file with a publication date, a retrieval date is not included in the APA reference list entry.
9. b. The word "Abstract" is included in brackets after the article title.
10. a. For a dissertation accessed from a database, the description "Doctoral dissertation" appears in parentheses following the title and the accession number is included at the end of the entry.

APA documentation, page 94

1. False. Although a page number is required for all quotations, it is not necessary for paraphrases and summaries except when providing one would help readers find the passage in a long work.
2. True. Because of these requirements, APA documentation style is sometimes called the "author/date" system.
3. True. The alphabetical organization helps readers quickly find the source that has been cited in the text.
4. False. An ampersand is used only in the parentheses following the citation; in a signal phrase, the word "and" is used.

5. True. Although some other documentation styles omit these abbreviations, APA requires them.
6. False. APA recommends using the past or the past perfect tense (for example, "Baker reported that" or "Wu has argued that").
7. True. The works are listed alphabetically by title, with the first work assigned "a," the second "b," and so on. In-text citations and the list of references both use this designation.
8. True. Because APA is a scientific style, dates are important; if no date is available, the fact must be noted.
9. False. In an APA reference list, "et al." is never used. If a work has eight or more authors, the names of the first six authors are given, followed by three ellipsis dots and the final author's name.
10. True. The title is used in place of the author's name unless "Anonymous" is actually given as the author in the source.

Thesis statements in *Chicago* (CMS) papers 1, page 95

1. a. This sentence can be developed into an argument about the importance of the discovery of anesthesia. The other sentence simply states a fact.
2. b. This sentence focuses on one famous explorer and makes an assertion that can be argued in a paper. The other sentence is too broad.
3. b. This sentence makes an assertion that can be developed into an argument about the value of film preservation. The other sentence simply states a fact.
4. a. This sentence makes a clear, focused point that can be argued in a paper. The other sentence is too vague to assert an arguable point.
5. a. This statement can be developed into an argument that explains why a government action in World War II was misguided. The other sentence simply states a fact.
6. a. This sentence makes an assertion for which evidence can be presented. The other sentence is too broad to be a useful thesis statement.
7. b. This sentence asserts an idea that can be argued in a paper. The other sentence is too factual.
8. b. This sentence presents an assertion for which evidence can be presented in a paper. The other sentence is too broad or factual to form the basis of an argument.
9. a. This sentence makes an assertion that can be argued in the paper. The other sentence merely states historical facts.
10. b. This sentence is focused, and it makes an arguable assertion. The other sentence is too broad because it covers many decades and hundreds of cities and towns.

Thesis statements in *Chicago* (CMS) papers 2, page 97

1. b. This statement sets up a cause-and-effect claim that can be supported with evidence in a paper. The other statement is too vague and speculative to be an effective thesis.
2. b. This statement presents an argument that can be developed and supported in a paper. The other statement merely defines what the Elgin marbles are; it is too factual to make an effective thesis.
3. a. This statement makes a claim that focuses on one particular president and the historical context of his scandal. The other statement is vague and too broad to make an effective thesis for a five-to-ten-page paper.
4. b. This statement makes an assertion about what made the American perspective change. The other statement is too factual to be an effective thesis.
5. a. This statement makes an assertion about the missionaries and sets up an argument that can be supported with

evidence in a paper. The other statement is too broad to be an effective thesis.

6. b. This statement makes a claim about the nuns that can be supported with evidence in a paper. The other statement is too factual to be an effective thesis.

7. b. This statement makes an assertion about the success of the Chinese Communist Party that can be supported with evidence in a paper. The other statement is too factual to be an effective thesis.

8. a. This statement makes an assertion about US preparedness that can be supported with evidence in a paper. The other statement is too vague to be an effective thesis.

9. b. This statement makes an assertion about the British withdrawal that can be supported with evidence in a paper. The other statement is too vague to be an effective thesis.

10. b. This statement makes an assertion about the protests that can be supported with evidence in a paper. The other statement is too factual to be an effective thesis.

Avoiding plagiarism in *Chicago* (CMS) papers 1, page 99

1. Plagiarized. Although the student has correctly documented the source with a footnote, the student has paraphrased the source too closely.

2. OK. The student has used quotation marks to indicate exact words from the source and has included a footnote.

3. OK. The student has paraphrased without using language or structure from the source and has cited the source with a footnote.

4. Plagiarized. The student has quoted part of the sentence word-for-word without using quotation marks.

5. Plagiarized. The student has quoted the source word-for-word without using quotation marks and has failed to name the author and provide a footnote.

6. OK. The student has paraphrased without using language or structure from the source and has cited the source with a footnote.

7. OK. The student has paraphrased without using language or structure from the source and has cited the source with a footnote.

8. Plagiarized. The student has used words from the source without quotation marks (*combined the two strands, lethal cocktail*) and has not cited the source in a footnote.

9. OK. The student has placed exact words from the source in quotation marks and has paraphrased other ideas from the source and documented the source with a footnote.

10. Plagiarized. The student has used the structure of the source and has simply plugged in synonyms for the words of the source (*beginnings* for *origins, the concentration camps* for *Auschwitz, seen* for *traced, momentous combination* for *fateful coupling*).

Avoiding plagiarism in *Chicago* (CMS) papers 2, page 101

1. OK. In addition to documenting the source with a footnote, the student has enclosed exact words from the source in quotation marks.

2. Plagiarized. Although the student has documented the source with a footnote, the student has used language from the source without enclosing it in quotation marks.

3. Plagiarized. The student has copied much of the sentence word-for-word from the source without using quotation marks.

4. OK. In addition to documenting the source with a footnote, the student has paraphrased it without borrowing its language or structure.

5. Plagiarized. Although the sentence ends with a note, the student has paraphrased the original source far too closely, borrowing structure from the original and plugging in synonyms (*failed to fire* for *jammed, pliant* for *soft, bent out of shape* for *deformed,* and so on).

6. OK. In addition to documenting the source, the student has paraphrased it without borrowing its language or structure.

7. Plagiarized. Although the sentence ends with a note, the student has copied a long phrase from the source word-for-word without using quotation marks (*Custer's troops used ammunition belts made from scrap leather*).

8. OK. In addition to documenting the source, the student has paraphrased it without borrowing its language or structure.

9. Plagiarized. After the introductory clause, the student has copied the source word-for-word without using quotation marks and has failed to provide a footnote to document the source.

10. OK. In addition to documenting the source with a footnote, the student has placed borrowed language in quotation marks and has used brackets around words that do not appear in the original source.

Avoiding plagiarism in *Chicago* (CMS) papers 3, page 103

1. OK. The student has paraphrased without using language or structure from the source.

2. Plagiarized. The student has borrowed phrases (*depended on its dogs, from the beginning*) from the source without enclosing them in quotation marks.

3. Plagiarized. The student has borrowed words from the source and rearranged them but has not indicated the borrowing with quotation marks.

4. OK. The student has enclosed exact language from the source in quotation marks.

5. Plagiarized. The writer's paraphrase uses the structure of the source's sentence while simply substituting synonyms for most words (*canine* for *dog, haul* for *pull, taken secretly* for *kidnapped*).

Avoiding plagiarism in *Chicago* (CMS) papers 4, page 104

1. Plagiarized. The student has used the exact language of the source (*had killed him with poisoned mushrooms*) without enclosing the words in quotation marks. In addition, the phrase *most likely but not quite certain* is too close to the language of the source to be an acceptable paraphrase.

2. OK. The student has paraphrased ideas from the source without borrowing language or sentence structure.

3. OK. The student has used quotation marks to enclose exact words from the source.

4. Plagiarized. The student has paraphrased the source too closely, using the sentence structure of the source and substituting synonyms for the language of the source (*prepared the way* for *cleared the ground, needed only to bide her time* for *only had to wait*).

5. OK. The student has paraphrased ideas without borrowing language or structure from the source.

Recognizing common knowledge in *Chicago* (CMS) papers, page 105

1. Common knowledge. This was a widely covered occurrence in modern history that continues to make news. It needs no citation.

2. Needs citation. This information is likely to be found only in a narrow range of sources; it may not be known even to some well-informed students of history. The source should be cited.

3. Common knowledge. Information about the life and death of a well-known figure is often common knowledge. The circumstances of Lincoln's assassination in particular have been exhaustively reported.

4. Needs citation. This is specific information about a subject unfamiliar to many readers, so the source should be cited.

5. Needs citation. The eruption of the volcano on Krakatau might be considered common knowledge, but specific information about the effects of the eruption should be cited.

6. Common knowledge. This general information about the Vietnam era appears in many sources, so no citation is required.

7. Common knowledge. This information would appear in any source about the Hillary expedition, which is credited as the first successful ascent of Everest. A well-known fact about a famous event needs no citation.

8. Common knowledge. This is a widely publicized fact about the life of a well-known general. Widely publicized information about famous figures in history generally needs no citation.

9. Common knowledge. This kind of general information about the underground railroad does not need to be cited.

10. Needs citation. This information is likely to come from a narrow range of sources. Because of the specificity of this statement, the writer should cite the source.

Integrating sources in *Chicago* (CMS) papers 1, page 107

1. OK. The student uses a signal phrase and places the exact words of the source in quotation marks.

2. This sentence is unacceptable. The student has put words in quotation marks that are slightly different from the words in the source. The following is an acceptable revision:
   > According to Barbara Hanawalt, "Practices associated with normal births in medieval Europe are shrouded in secrecy." 2

3. The passage is unacceptable. The second sentence is a dropped quotation. The student has failed to provide a signal phrase naming the author. The following is an acceptable revision:
   > "Practices associated with normal births in medieval Europe are shrouded in secrecy," Barbara Hanawalt notes, "not because the births were hidden at the time, but because they were a woman's ritual and women did not pass on information about them in writing." 3

4. OK. The student has smoothly integrated quoted words from the source into the sentence. The student also has introduced the quotation with a signal phrase and enclosed it in quotation marks.

5. OK. The student has enclosed exact words from the source in quotation marks and has used an ellipsis mark to show where words have been omitted.

6. The passage is unacceptable. The student has correctly indented the long quotation from the source but should not have used quotation marks around the indented quotation. In addition, an indented quotation should be introduced by a complete sentence, usually followed by a colon. The following is an acceptable revision:
   > Barbara Hanawalt notes that little information has come down to us about normal births in the Middle Ages:

Practices associated with normal births in medieval Europe are shrouded in secrecy, not because the births were hidden at the time, but because they were a woman's ritual and women did not pass on information about them in writing. Indeed, we can be quite sure that the event of a birth was well known within the immediate community. Living close together, the neighbors would hear the cries of a woman in labor and would observe the midwife and female friends gathering around. But what occurred in the birthing chamber was not known to the men listening outside, and so it was not recorded. 6

7. This passage is unacceptable. The student has omitted material between the two sentences that appear in quotation marks and has failed to indicate the omission with an ellipsis mark. The following is an acceptable revision:
   > Little is known today about normal births in the Middle Ages. Barbara Hanawalt explains that births "were a woman's ritual and women did not pass on information about them in writing. . . . But what occurred in the birthing chamber was not known to the men listening outside, and so it was not recorded." 7

8. OK. The student has enclosed exact words from the source in quotation marks and has used brackets to indicate an addition that clarifies the quoted material.

9. This passage is unacceptable. The material in quotation marks is a dropped quotation. The student has enclosed the words of the source in quotation marks but has not used a signal phrase identifying the author and has not provided enough context for the quotation. The following is an acceptable revision:
   > Only abnormal births are described in learned medieval writings. Barbara Hanawalt explains why: "Male doctors never attended a normal birth, so they knew nothing about them. They were called in only when surgery was needed." 9

10. OK. The student has smoothly integrated the quotation into the sentence and has introduced it with a signal phrase.

Integrating sources in *Chicago* (CMS) papers 2, page 109

1. OK. The student has enclosed words from the source in quotation marks and has named the author in a signal phrase.

2. The sentence is unacceptable. This sentence contains a dropped quotation. The student has failed to provide a signal phrase naming the author. The following is an acceptable revision:
   > In the Anglo-French wars prior to 1815, historian Kennedy points out, "victory . . . went to the Power—or better, since both Britain and France usually had allies, to the Great Power coalition—with the greater capacity to maintain credit and to keep on raising supplies." 2

3. This sentence is unacceptable. The student has left out words from the source (*would look to a more powerful ally for loans and reinforcements in order to*) but has not indicated the omission with an ellipsis mark. In addition, the student has added the word *could*, which is not in the source, without putting brackets around it. The following is an acceptable revision:
   > Kennedy notes that in the wars between Britain and France before 1815, the key to victory was building a coalition of countries so that "a belligerent whose resources were fading . . . [could] keep itself in the fight." 3

4. OK. The student has quoted the source correctly and has enclosed borrowed words in quotation marks.
5. OK. The student has put the exact words of the source in quotation marks and has used ellipsis marks to indicate omissions from the source. The student also has used brackets to enclose a word that makes the quotation fit within the grammar of the sentence.

Chicago (CMS) documentation: identifying elements of sources, page 111

1. a. In *Chicago* style for a work with three authors, all authors' names are given in full.
2. a. *Chicago* style uses the abbreviation "no.," not a period, before the issue number.
3. b. The *Chicago* bibliography entry should include the title of the entire work as well as the number and title of the volume.
4. a. The volume and issue numbers are given. Only the first page of the article is given in the database listing, so the page number is followed by a plus sign in the bibliography entry.
5. a. The database record does not give a DOI, so in *Chicago* style, the bibliography entry should end with the database name.
6. b. The name of the author of the work appears first, and the words "Translated by" are spelled out following the title.
7. a. The name of the reviewer should appear first, followed by the title of the review, the words "Review of," and then the title of the work reviewed and the author of the work.
8. a. In *Chicago* style for a magazine, the date should be given in month-day-year order with the month spelled out.
9. a. The position of the Library of Congress at the top of the page and at the bottom left indicates that it is the sponsor.
10. b. The website title and the sponsor of the site are given after the title of the document.

Chicago (CMS) documentation: notes 1, page 117

1. a. In a *Chicago* note, the names of all authors appear in normal order, first name first.
2. b. When a source has been previously cited, the note should appear in shortened form. Only the last name of the author, a shortened form of the title (in this case the whole title because it is only four words), and a page number are required.
3. b. For two consecutive notes from the same source, give the author's last name, a short form of the title, and the page or pages cited.
4. a. In a *Chicago* note, commas (not periods) are used after the author's name and after the title of the article.
5. b. The exact date of a weekly magazine must be given in the note.
6. b. A shortened form of the title (in this case the full title because it is only two words) should be set off with commas, not with parentheses, and the author's last name, not first and last, should be used.
7. a. For a work with two authors, both authors' names must be given; "and others" is used only when a work has four or more authors. (And a translator is not counted in the list of authors.)
8. b. The note begins with the name of the person interviewed.
9. a. The note includes the URL for the article.
10. b. The note for an online article includes the volume and issue numbers if available.

Chicago (CMS) documentation: notes 2, page 121

1. b. In a *Chicago* note, the name of the author appears in normal order, first name first.
2. a. When a source has been previously cited, only the last name of the author, a shortened form of the title, and a page number are required.
3. a. Both authors' last names are given, even in a shortened note.
4. a. Commas, not periods, separate the elements in a *Chicago* note.
5. b. A work with an unknown author is cited by its title.
6. b. The title of the full website is included after the title of the short document.
7. a. A note for a magazine article includes only the date, not the volume and issue numbers.
8. b. In a *Chicago* note for a newspaper article, the section letter or number, not the page number, is cited.
9. a. For two consecutive notes from the same page in the same source, give the author's last name, a short form of the title, and the page or pages cited.
10. b. The note includes the sponsor of the site, National Public Radio, as well as the title of the site (NPR).

Chicago (CMS) documentation: notes 3, page 125

1. b. In a *Chicago* note, the names of all authors are given first name first.
2. b. In *Chicago* note style, all months of the year are spelled out in full.
3. b. In *Chicago* style, all dates are given in month-day-year order.
4. a. In *Chicago* style, the word "in" comes after the title of the short work and before the title of the collection.
5. a. *Chicago* note style does not use angle brackets around URLs.
6. b. In a *Chicago* note, the title of the online magazine precedes the date of posting.
7. a. In *Chicago* style, a note for a work without an author begins with the title of the work.
8. a. A note for a review includes only the title and author, not complete publishing information, for the work reviewed.
9. b. A note for a source cited earlier in the paper gives the author's last name and a short title of the source.
10. a. For a later reference to a source you have already cited, use the author's last name, a short title, and the page or pages cited.

Chicago (CMS) documentation: bibliography 1, page 129

1. b. In a *Chicago* bibliography entry, the author's name is given last name first.
2. a. In a *Chicago* bibliography entry, all authors' names are given for works with two or more authors.
3. b. In a *Chicago* bibliography entry for a journal article, the year in parentheses follows the volume and issue numbers.
4. a. Only the date and page numbers are given for a magazine article in a *Chicago* bibliography.
5. a. In *Chicago* bibliography style, the term "edited by" is spelled out in full before the editor's name.
6. b. The word "unpublished" is not used in a *Chicago* bibliography entry. The quotation marks indicate that the dissertation is unpublished.
7. b. In a *Chicago* bibliography entry, the sponsor of the website is given in addition to the title of the site.

8. a. For an article accessed through a database, *Chicago* requires a persistent or stable URL if one is listed and if no DOI is listed.
9. b. A *Chicago* bibliography entry for an online article includes the name and date of the publication, as for a print article.
10. a. A bibliography entry for a film begins with the director's name followed by the name of the film.

Chicago (CMS) documentation: bibliography 2, page 133

1. b. A *Chicago* bibliography entry for a newspaper article gives the section letter, not the page number.
2. a. In a *Chicago* bibliography entry for an essay appearing in an anthology, the author of the essay is listed first, followed by the essay title, the anthology title, and the editor of the anthology.
3. b. A *Chicago* bibliography entry for a book review lists the name of the reviewer first and the name of the book's author after the title of the book.
4. b. A *Chicago* bibliography entry for a journal citation includes the year as well as the volume and issue number.
5. b. In a *Chicago* bibliography entry for a letter in a collection, the date of the letter is month-day-year.
6. a. For a work from a website in a *Chicago* bibliography, the date of access is included if the source itself has no date.
7. b. Information about a discussion list posting is included only in a note, not in the bibliography.
8. b. A *Chicago* bibliography entry for a book does not include page numbers. Page numbers are included in a note.
9. a. A *Chicago* bibliography entry for a movie begins with the director's name (or directors' names) and includes both the dates of original release and the date and format viewed by the student.
10. a. If there is no DOI, a *Chicago* bibliography entry for an article found in a database ends with the name of the database.

Chicago (CMS) documentation: bibliography 3, page 137

1. a. In *Chicago* bibliography entries, the first author's name is reversed, but subsequent names are listed in normal order.
2. b. In a *Chicago* bibliography entry for a website with no named author, the entry begins with the title.
3. a. When two sources in a *Chicago* bibliography are by the same author, the sources are listed alphabetically by title.

4. b. Email messages are treated like personal communications and are not included in the bibliography.
5. b. In a *Chicago* bibliography entry for a film on DVD, the director/writer is listed first and the original release date of the film, if known, is listed before the DVD distribution information.
6. a. In a *Chicago* bibliography entry for a source quoted in another source, the publication information for the original source is required.
7. a. A *Chicago* bibliography entry for an article accessed through an online database includes both print publication information and the stable URL for the article if there is no DOI.
8. a. In *Chicago* bibliography entries for journal articles, the volume and issue numbers are included along with the year.
9. b. In a *Chicago* bibliography entry for a newspaper article, the section letter, if available, is sufficient; a page number is not included.
10. a. In a *Chicago* bibliography entry for a work with three or more authors, all authors' names are listed.

Chicago (CMS) documentation, page 140

1. True. Notes are required for summaries and paraphrases as well as for quotations.
2. False. The bibliography may include both the works cited in the notes and works the writer consulted but did not cite.
3. False. A note is needed for each reference to a source; abbreviated notes are used for subsequent references to a source.
4. False. For two consecutive notes from the same source, give the author's last name, a short form of the title, and the page number or numbers cited.
5. True. The bibliography is organized alphabetically so that readers can quickly find the source cited in the paper.
6. False. *Chicago* style does not require angle brackets around a URL.
7. True. The note format and the bibliography format differ slightly.
8. False. Notes begin with a paragraph-style indent, but in the bibliography each entry begins against the left margin, and any additional lines are indented.
9. True. Either footnotes or endnotes are acceptable.
10. False. Note numbers in the text of the paper appear in superscript (they are slightly raised above the line of text). The numbers are not enclosed in parentheses.

Acknowledgments

Jean Baudrillard, excerpt from *For a Critique of the Political Economy of the Sign* by Jean Baudrillard, trans. Charles Levin. Copyright © 1981 Telos Press Publishing. Reprinted with permission.

Beethoven, excerpt from "Ludwig van Beethoven (1770–1827), Symphony No. 9 in D minor, Opus 125." Boston Symphony Orchestra, May 3, 2012. Used by permission.

S. M. Bianchi, excerpt from "The more they change, the more they stay the same? Understanding family change in the twenty-first century." *Contemporary Sociology*, 42(3), 324–331.

Reprinted by permission of SAGE Publications, Inc.; permission conveyed through Copyright Clearance Center, Inc.

The Pew Charitable Trusts, excerpt from *Collateral Costs: Incarceration's Effect on Economic Mobility*, 6–8. © The Pew Charitable Trusts.

Scientific American, table of contents page from *Scientific American* 292, no. 5 (May 2005): 6. Copyright © 2005 Scientific American, a division of Nature America, Inc. All rights reserved. This page includes images by Matt Collins, copyright © Matt Collins, reprinted by permission, and an image by Flynn Larsen, copyright © Flynn Larsen, reprinted by permission.

For Julia

Text copyright © 2003 by Shirley Glaser

Illustrations copyright © 2003 by Milton Glaser

Thanks to Katja Maas for making magic.

First Edition

1 3 5 7 10 8 6 4 2

Printed in Singapore

This book is set in Bauer Bodoni, Franklin
Gothic, Frutiger, News Gothic, and
Snell Roundhand.

ISBN 0-7868-0865-9

Library of Congress information on file.

Visit www.hyperionchildrensbooks.com

The Alphazeds

WORDS BY
Shirley Glaser

PICTURES BY
Milton Glaser

Miramax Books
Hyperion Books for Children
New York

A long time ago, before there was anything, there was a small empty yellow room.

HI!

Suddenly, out of nowhere, a fat pink-and-green thorny leg burst through the doorway. It belonged to Angry A—the first Alphazed.

EXCUSE ME...

WHAT ARE YOU DOING HERE?

A moment later, A was followed into the room by Bashful B.

TA-DA!

Right after Bashful B, Confused C and Dynamic D came in.

I'M NOT SURE I WAS INVITED!

WHAT'S YOUR NAME?

B.

WHO INVITED YOU HERE?.

I DON'T BELIEVE THAT IS ANY OF YOUR CONCERN.

TA-DA!

A moment later, Elegant E entered.

WOULD YOU EXCUSE ME, PLEASE?

IS IT TOO EARLY TO LEAVE?

Flamboyant F arrived with a flourish.

HOW ABOUT A DANCE, SKINNY!

I DON'T DANCE.

NEITHER DO I.

CERTAINLY NOT!

Suddenly there was a loud groaning noise at the doorway that frightened the Alphazeds.

WHAT IS THAT THING?

HOW WOULD I KNOW— I JUST GOT HERE.

MY WORD!

HELP!

GASP!

TA-DA!

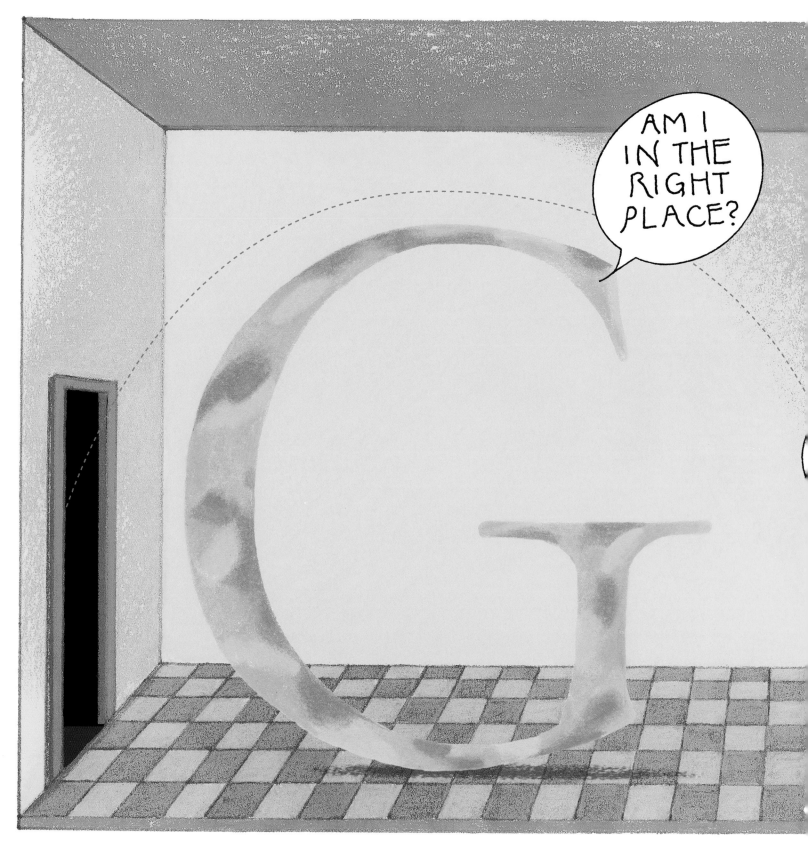

Speech bubble: AM I IN THE RIGHT PLACE?

Gigantic G squeezed in as Hopping H hip-hopped over him.

HUP, HUP, OUT OF MY WAY, FOLKS!

I WISH I WERE TALLER.

YOU'RE EXACTLY THE RIGHT SIZE AS FAR AS I'M CONCERNED.

The next three Alphazeds, Italic I, Jealous J, and Kicking K, arrived together.

WATCH OUT BELOW! WATCH OUT BELOW! YA KNOW WHAT I'M SAYIN'?

ME TOO!

I AM WATCHING, YOU SILLY THING!

HOW MUCH DOES A GUY LIKE YOU WEIGH?

ARE YOU IN ANY WAY RELATED TO A ?

I JUST FOLLOWED HIM.

I DUNNO.

TA-DA!

YOU CALL THAT DRESSED UP?

YOU DON'T LOOK SO TOUGH TO ME.

AM I THE ONLY ONE WHO BOTHERED TO GET DRESSED UP?

DON'T PUSH IT!

NO!

I WISH I WERE AS GOOD-LOOKING AS YOU.

OH, THANK YOU.

Lovely L, Mighty M, and Negative N came in, followed by Ornate O.

OW! OW! YA KNOW WHAT I'M SAYIN'?

I HAVE NO IDEA WHAT'S HAPPENING.

I DARE SAY, IT'S GETTING A BIT CROWD-ED.

I'M INCLINED TO LEAVE SOON.

WHY DID YOU KICK H?

HE BUGS ME.

ME, TOO.

TA-DA!

CAN I FIT IN HERE?

OH M, OH MY, OH DEAR.

BE OF GOOD CHEER R IS HERE.

PAS POSSIBLE.

I WISH I WERE FLEXIBLE LIKE YOU.

I NEVER GET INVITED TO PARTIES.

SSS...

By now the room had become quite crowded and noisy. Pretentious P, Quaking Q, Rhyming R, and Sibilant S piled into the room below Towering T, stepping over little Unimportant U.

I THINK I MAY HAVE BEEN HERE IN ANOTHER LIFE.

GET OUT OF MY WAY YOU BIG GALOOT!

I DON'T KNOW IF I CAN TOLERATE MUCH MORE OF THIS...

I'M FLYIN! I'M FLYIN! YA' KNOW WHAT I'M SAYIN'?

WANT TO ARM WRESTLE?

I'D CRUSH YOU.

OUCH!

TA-DA!

WHO ARE ALL THESE STRANGE CHARACTERS?

-I-I -DON'T KNOW N-AN-AN- ANYBODY HERE.

NO.

I'M FAMISHED.

I'M GLAD I'M NOT SHORT... THE AIR MUST BE AWFUL DOWN THERE.

JUST HOPPIN' ALONG! JUST HOPPIN' ALONG! YA KNOW WHAT I'M SAYIN'?

I THINK SOMETHING IS ABOUT TO HAPPEN.

I'M INCLINED TO AGREE.

SHOULD I COME IN OR GO OUT?

PERHAPS.

IS EVERYONE TALKING ABOUT ME?

I WISH I HAD A VOICE LIKE YOURS.

GET ME OUTA HERE!

I DON'T LIKE ANYONE HERE.

ME, NEITHER.

SSS...

Vain V, Wise W, Xenophobic X, and Yelling Y all pushed in just before Zigzag Z, always the last to arrive.

The noise was terrible. Everyone was screaming at the top of their lungs. Nobody cared about anyone else. They were pushing and shoving and hitting and kicking. It was a disaster. . . .

Suddenly . . .

The light went out, and darkness filled the room. After a time of the deepest silence, a voice was heard.

"Let there be light."

When the light came back on, something extraordinary had happened. Four letters had gotten together to comfort one another. Together they had managed to create something larger and more important than themselves. *They had made the first word.* At that moment, all the letters suddenly realized their reason for being in the room. It wasn't simply about expressing themselves or showing off. They could be a part of something bigger, something that mattered. They could work together, and everyone could play an important part.

TA-DA!

In the beginning there was the WORD.

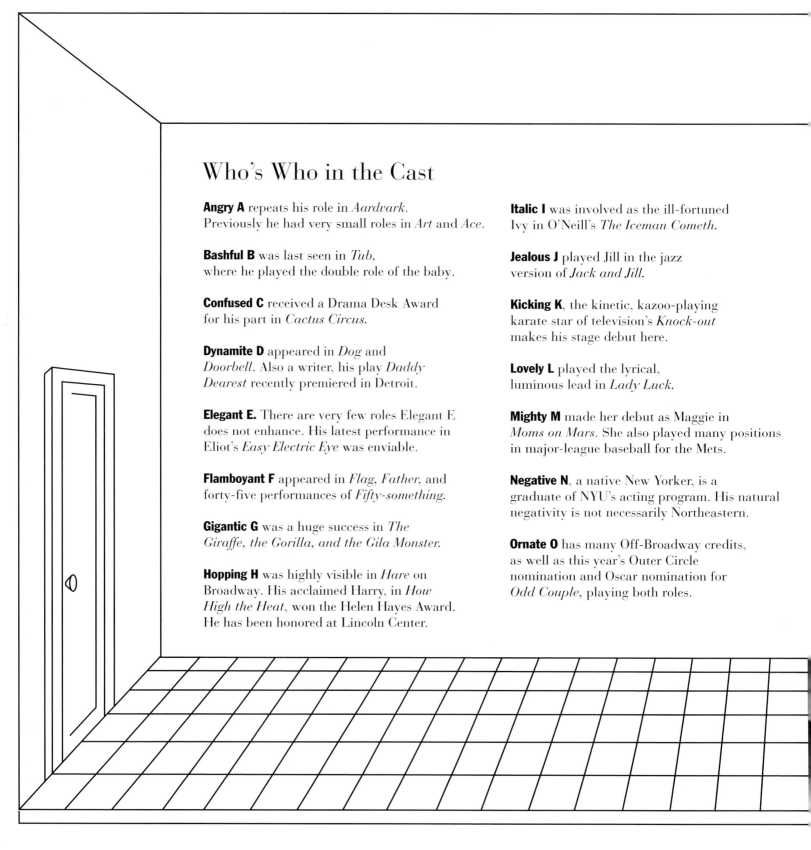

Who's Who in the Cast

Angry A repeats his role in *Aardvark*. Previously he had very small roles in *Art* and *Ace*.

Bashful B was last seen in *Tub*, where he played the double role of the baby.

Confused C received a Drama Desk Award for his part in *Cactus Circus*.

Dynamite D appeared in *Dog* and *Doorbell*. Also a writer, his play *Daddy Dearest* recently premiered in Detroit.

Elegant E. There are very few roles Elegant E does not enhance. His latest performance in Eliot's *Easy Electric Eye* was enviable.

Flamboyant F appeared in *Flag*, *Father*, and forty-five performances of *Fifty-something*.

Gigantic G was a huge success in *The Giraffe, the Gorilla, and the Gila Monster*.

Hopping H was highly visible in *Hare* on Broadway. His acclaimed Harry, in *How High the Heat*, won the Helen Hayes Award. He has been honored at Lincoln Center.

Italic I was involved as the ill-fortuned Ivy in O'Neill's *The Iceman Cometh*.

Jealous J played Jill in the jazz version of *Jack and Jill*.

Kicking K, the kinetic, kazoo-playing karate star of television's *Knock-out* makes his stage debut here.

Lovely L played the lyrical, luminous lead in *Lady Luck*.

Mighty M made her debut as Maggie in *Moms on Mars*. She also played many positions in major-league baseball for the Mets.

Negative N, a native New Yorker, is a graduate of NYU's acting program. His natural negativity is not necessarily Northeastern.

Ornate O has many Off-Broadway credits, as well as this year's Outer Circle nomination and Oscar nomination for *Odd Couple*, playing both roles.

The Alphazeds are all around us. The ones in this book are based on real characters that belong to typographic families, with curious names—look for them.

Aurora   Bodoni   Corinthian   Dynamo   Excelsior   Fraktur   Garamond Book   Hobo   Isbell Medium Italic   Jim Crow   Korinna   Lafayette   Mastodon   News Gothic

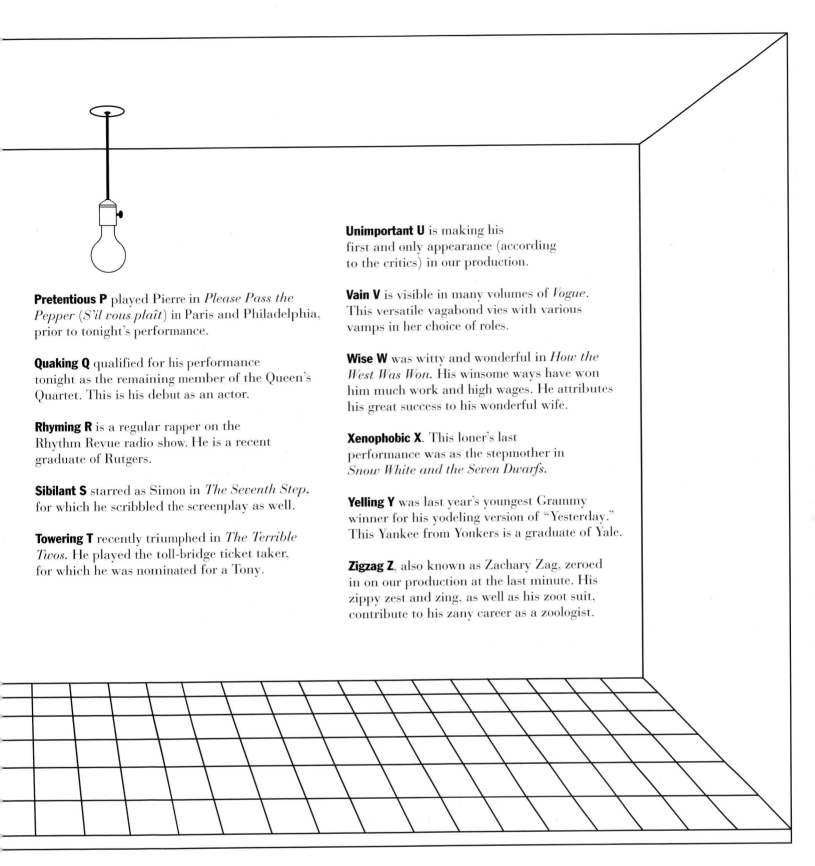

Pretentious P played Pierre in *Please Pass the Pepper* (*S'il vous plaît*) in Paris and Philadelphia, prior to tonight's performance.

Quaking Q qualified for his performance tonight as the remaining member of the Queen's Quartet. This is his debut as an actor.

Rhyming R is a regular rapper on the Rhythm Revue radio show. He is a recent graduate of Rutgers.

Sibilant S starred as Simon in *The Seventh Step*, for which he scribbled the screenplay as well.

Towering T recently triumphed in *The Terrible Twos*. He played the toll-bridge ticket taker, for which he was nominated for a Tony.

Unimportant U is making his first and only appearance (according to the critics) in our production.

Vain V is visible in many volumes of *Vogue*. This versatile vagabond vies with various vamps in her choice of roles.

Wise W was witty and wonderful in *How the West Was Won*. His winsome ways have won him much work and high wages. He attributes his great success to his wonderful wife.

Xenophobic X. This loner's last performance was as the stepmother in *Snow White and the Seven Dwarfs*.

Yelling Y was last year's youngest Grammy winner for his yodeling version of "Yesterday." This Yankee from Yonkers is a graduate of Yale.

Zigzag Z, also known as Zachary Zag, zeroed in on our production at the last minute. His zippy zest and zing, as well as his zoot suit, contribute to his zany career as a zoologist.

Ornate Wood Perpetua Quorum Black Romana Bold A Snake Torino Universe 75 Venus Extra Bold Weiss Roman Bold Xerxes Yagi Link Double Zapf Medium Italic

LEBANON VALLEY COLLEGE LIBRARY

Lebanon Valley College
Bishop Library
Annville, PA 17003

GAYLORD RG